Reprint Series No. 1

CROCHET DESIGNS

Fashions & Accessories

Reprinted from

Victorian and Edwardian Sources

Compiled by

Gertrude Kuehl

for the

Knitting and Crochet Guild

KNITTING AND CROCHET GUILD

London

1990

ACKNOWLEDGEMENTS

The Knitting and Crochet Guild wishes to express its deep appreciation to Lady Scott, Patron of the Guild, for her encouragement and generous support, without which the work could not have been completed. Many other members of the Guild have contributed to the project through their interest in crochet work and its history, and we can name only a few who have made special contributions of their time, experience and skills: Margaret Deshmane, Sue Leighton-White, Jo Olley, Sheila Ryle, Anita Schuetz, Barbara Tennant, Mavis Walker and all those who have kindly agreed to crochet designs for exhibition.

First published in Great Britain in 1990
by the Knitting and Crochet Guild
47 Yarmouth Rd., Ormesby St. Margaret
Great Yarmouth, Norfolk NR29 3QE
Charity registration No. 802465

The designs contained in this book have been
reprinted in facsimile from the original
sources quoted in the Table of Contents.
Part of the intrinsic interest of these historic
designs is their original presentation and in the
interests of authenticity these designs have been
reproduced directly from the originals without comment
or amendment. No responsibility, therefore, can be
accepted for any errors existing in the original designs.
It should also be noted that any defects in the standard
of reproduction reflect those of the original sources.

To the best of our knowledge
all of the material reprinted is no longer
under copyright. We apologise, therefore,
for any copyright infringement which might
occur, which is purely inadvertent.

British Library Cataloguing in Publication Data
Crochet designs : fashions & accessories : reprinted from
Victorian and Edwardian sources.
1. Crocheting, history
I. Kuehl, Gertrude   II. Knitting and Crochet Guild
III. Series
746. 43409

ISBN 0-9513491-1-2

Printed in Great Britain by Crowes Printers, 11 Concorde Road,
Norwich NR6 6BJ.

CONTENTS

Hook size comparison chart

METRIC (ISR) SIZES in mm.	VICTORIAN BELL GAUGE SIZES (steel, bone, ivory, celluloid, wood)	PRE-METRIC BRITISH SIZES as represented by Abel Morrall Redditch ("Aero") "cotton" (steel)	"wool" (aluminium, & plastic)	PRE-METRIC BRITISH SIZES as represented by Henry Milward & Sons Studley "cotton" (steel)	"wool" (aluminium & plastic)	MODERN U.S. HOOK SIZES Letters in () = old US letter sizes "cotton" (steel)	"wool" (aluminium, plastic, wood)
10.00							P & 15* (P) *
9.00							13* (O) M & 13†
8.00							N & 11* (N) L & 11†
7.00	1 2	1 2	1 2	1 2			(M) K & 10½
6.00	3 4	3 4	3 4	3 4			(L) I & 10† (K) J & 10
5.50	5	5	5	5			I & 9
5.00	6	6	6	6			(J) H & 8
4.50	7	7	7	7			(I) G & 7
4.00	8	8	8	8		6	(H) F
3.50	9	9	9	9			(G) E & 4
3.00	10 11	000	10	000	10 11	00	(F) 3 (E) D
2.50	12	00 0	11 12	00	12	0 1	2 (D) C
2.00	13 14	1 1½	13 14	0 1	13 14	2 3 4	(C) 1 (B) B & 0
1.75	15 16	2 2½		1½ 2		5 6 7	
1.50	17	3 3½		2½		8	
1.25	18	4 4½		3		9 10	
1.00	19 20	5 5½		3½ 4		11 12	
.75	21 22	6 6½		4½ 5		13	
.60	23 24	7		5½ 6		14	
	25	7½		6½		15	
	26	8		7		16	
	27			8			
	28			9			

* plastic
† wood

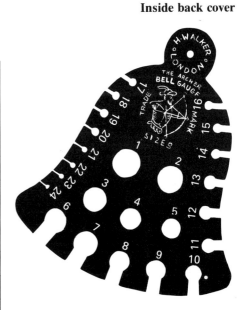

Walker's Bell Gauge
These gauges were used to measure the size of knitting needles, netting-meshes, and crochet hooks. Knitting needles and netting meshes were measured simply by slipping them into the holes or slits, as they are of equal diameter throughout their length. Crochet hooks, however, should be measured by slipping the **widest** part of the hook head itself into the narrow **channel** leading to the rounded holes around the edge of the gauge, except for the largest hooks (nos. 1 – 5) which were measured by inserting the hook through the holes in the centre of the gauge.

FOREWORD

The Knitting and Crochet Guild has entered the decade of the 1990s with new responsibilities as a registered charity and with renewed dedication to promoting excellence and keeping alive for the younger generation the skills of crochet and machine and hand knitting. The Guild's educational work has always involved preserving the best of the old while exploring the new, and to this end the Guild has reprinted crochet designs from historical sources which reflect developments in the craft during the second half of the 19th and early 20th centuries.

By focussing on women's fashions, these reprinted designs illustrate how crochet was used by previous generations to enhance many aspects of a woman's wardrobe, and now these Victorian and Edwardian designs can provide inspiration for the modern woman to use crochet in contemporary fashion.

I believe there is much in these designs to stimulate interest among students, teachers, designers, and the casual crocheter — all of whom will find new ideas to adapt to modern fashion needs.

Anne Scott

Lady Scott

YARN CATEGORIES

NOTE: These are examples for your guidance only. Victorian/Edwardian designs should be worked-to-measure (see introduction), taking account of the weight & texture of the yarn chosen, the hook size, and your individual tension as a crocheter (tight or loose), to achieve the desired result. This requires more study and sample-working, but paves the way for successful yarn substitution.

GENERAL CATEGORIES OF YARNS AND THREADS	EXAMPLES OF TYPES OF OLD YARNS AND THREADS This list includes some yarns/threads which are not mentioned in the designs in this book, in order to give a general over-view of early yarns and threads.	EXAMPLES OF TYPES OF MODERN YARNS AND THREADS	SUGGESTED METRIC HOOK SIZES (A design may require an unusually large hook for a lacey effect: or a smaller hook for a firm fabric.)
EXTRA FINE WEIGHT	– non mercerised cotton (eg Coats 24-50*) – mercerised cotton (eg Coats 60-150*) – very fine silk and linen threads	– fine mercerised cotton (no. 60 upward) – very fine silk & linen lace thread	.60 – .75
VERY FINE WEIGHT	– non-mercerised cotton (eg Coats 8-22*) – mercerised cotton (eg Coats 10-50*) – Star Sylko no. 12 – purse silk – Pyrenean wool	– mercerised cotton nos. 10-40 – 1-ply Shetland "cob-web" wool	1.00 – 1.50
FINE WEIGHT	– Silver Shield crochet thread – Strutts macrame twine no 8 – non-mercerised cotton (cg Coats 00-8*) – mercerised cotton (eg Coats 1-10*) – Star sylko nos. 3 & 5 – Beehive Ivorine – Shetland floss	– Lyscordet cotton – Pearl cotton no. 8 & 5 – 2-ply Shetland lace wt. wool – standard 2-ply baby yarns – standard 2-ply machine knitting yarns	1.75 – 2.50
LIGHT WEIGHT	– Lady Betty fleecy – Andalusian wool – Eider 2-ply wool – Berlin fingerings for baby wear – single Berlin wool** – 4-ply fingering (best quality)	– standard 3-ply yarns – standard 4-ply yarns – soft cottons	3.00 – 4.00
MEDIUM WEIGHT	– double Berlin wool** – 2-ply fleecy wool – petticoat wool	– standard double knitting yarns – dishcloth cotton	4.00 – 5.50
HEAVY WEIGHT	– 5-ply Scotch fingering – 3-ply wheeling (Alloa yarn) – 3-ply cable fleecy – Leviathan 12-ply fleecy	– Aran yarns – triple knitting yarns	6.00 – 8.00
BULKY/ CHUNKY WEIGHT	– Smyrna rug yarn – Kurdistan rug yarn – Parisian wool yarn	– rug yarns – chunky knits – Icelandic Lopi	8.00 – 10.00
NOVELTY OR UNUSUALLY TEXTURED	– Astrakhan yarn – Karakul (Carakul) yarn – feather wool – Ostrich wool	– slubbed and boucle yarns – poodle yarns	SELECT HOOK TO SUIT UNUSUAL CHARACTERISTICS OF THE YARN

*Details of J & P Coats' crochet thread sizes showing early 20th century mercerised thread sizes and the equivalent "ordinary crochet" (non-mercerised) cotton. Unfortunately many of these cotton numbers are no longer available.

MERCER-CROCHET	1	2	3	5	10	15	20	25	30	40	50	60	70	80	100	150
ORDINARY CROCHET	–	00	0	6	8	10	14	16	18	20	22	24	30	36	40	50

Taken from J & P Coats 3-fold pattern card leaflet no. 502 (c 1915) The same general sizing system was adopted by Arderns.

** Berlin wool was available in 4-ply 'single Berlin' and 8-ply 'double Berlin', and if a pattern simply stated Berlin wool without specifying the ply, it was the 4-ply single Berlin that was intended.

INTRODUCTION

For the crocheter who is prepared to undertake a little study and experimentation these designs will become a source of inspiration and delight. There have, of course, been many changes since these designs were created (the oldest was first published 142 years ago), and some background information may help in understanding and using them.

Terminology

When written patterns began to appear in publications of the mid-19th century, Victorian needlewomen were still in the process of inventing a written language to describe crochet techniques which had previously been taught by sample and example. It is small wonder then that there is some variation in the terms used to describe basic stitches and groups of stitch patterns. For example, some writers began by describing our treble crochet stitch as "long" because of the way it looked when compared with other stitches, while others described it by the three basic mechanical movements required to complete the stitch, hence, "triple" or "treble".

A number of outstandingly creative and dynamic needlewomen made important contributions to the development of crochet generally and in particular to the uniform terminology we have today. We have included two designs to illustrate the state of the art in the mid-19th century: a collar by Mdlle Eleanor Riego de La Branchardiere, and a coin purse by Mrs. Eliza Warren and Mrs. Matilda Pullan. Not only did these women produce a wide range of lace and fabric crochet designs, but each was active in publishing their own designs and editing women's magazines which featured needlework. Within a generation the efforts of such early crocheting pioneers and others led to a fair degree of uniformity in terminology, although some oddities persisted into the 20th century. Most of the designs contained in this book include explanations of any unusual stitches or procedures needed to work them, and the explanation of basic stitches at the front includes some additional information to help clarify terminology. Mary Konior's book *Heritage Crochet* (Dryad Press, 1987) discusses terminology and other aspects of early crochet.

Styles of pattern writing and methods of working

Generally speaking 19th century crochet patterns provide either a feast or a famine in written details. The earliest written patterns usually gave only the barest minimum of instruction focussing mainly on the particular stitch pattern to be used. Another example of economy in pattern writing were the charted designs developed for Berlin work (needlepoint on canvas) which were quickly adapted to filet crochet with a minimum of written instruction, and were also used for working solid crochet with coloured threads and for crocheted beadwork. But surprisingly by the 1880s pattern writing had moved to the opposite extreme, and the popular needlework magazine produced crochet patterns covering several pages of closely printed, repetitive instructions. Unfortunately this trend even affected instructions for filet crochet and the very useful squared charts virtually disappeard from use in this country. Despite the length of many late 19th and early 20th century crochet patterns, they still lacked some details commonly found in modern patterns. The modern crocheter has become accustomed to pattern instructions which designate a particular yarn or thread, a particular hook size and tension, and which give details for increases, decreases and finishing. Many Victorian/Edwardian patterns, however, did not have this particular focus or objective − they are in fact more "open-ended" to permit greater scope for adaptation. Such crochet instructions may seem uncomfortably vague to us, but Victorian needlewomen were accustomed to pattern cutting, dressmaking and fitting in the home (either their own efforts or those of an overworked, underpaid seamstress). It was assumed that crocheted garments would be tackled in the same way as dressmaking and it is not uncommon to find crochet patterns which remind the crocheter to cut and fit a paper pattern and to refer to it frequently for increasing and decreasing. Some women's magazines sold paper patterns specifically to accompany printed crochet instructions. In other words, these early crocheters thought first of the over-all outline of

the garment they wanted, then prepared a paper pattern cut to fit the measurements of the person for whom it was intended, and then proceeded to crochet the fabric required by *working to the pattern measurements*. Details of increases or decreases were often left to the expertise of the crocheter as she followed the outline of her paper pattern; or if such details were given, they were for only one size of garment. A specific yarn might be mentioned, particularly by the late 19th century as more reputable brand names appeared and were widely available; on the other hand, a pattern might simply suggest the use of a particular class of yarn, such as the popular Berlin wool. The size of hook might be mentioned, or a seemingly vague suggestion like "a coarse hook", or simply "choose a hook to suit the yarn". Bone, ivory or wooden hooks seldom carried a number, but were sized by using a hook and needle gauge, such as the popular Walker's bell gauge. Most, but not all, steel hooks were numbered by their manufacturers, but there was no overall standardisation and hook sizes varied from manufacturer to manufacturer, especially in the smaller sizes (see hook size chart).

It should be added that tension squares were used, or at least recommended by the pattern writers, but the rationale for the tension square was basically different from that of the modern printed pattern which is often written for a specific yarn. As the Victorian/Edwardian crocheter began by cutting a paper pattern (or using an existing cloth garment as a pattern), she needed the tension square (1) to provide a sample of the quality and other properties of the yarn or thread chosen (i.e. a test of elasticity, dye fastness, washability, etc); (2) to provide a sample of the crochet stitch pattern recommended by the instructions, to practice it and determine whether it was suitable for the yarn; (3) to select the right hook for working with the yarn, and for producing the type of fabric needed for the overall garment (loose and lacey for shawls or firm for slippers, etc.); and last, but by no means least (4) to provide the basic calculations for determining the number of stitches needed for the foundation chain and judging the subsequent increases and decreases needed for her measurements.

All of this placed greater demands on the Victorian/Edwardian crocheter. For those of us who have been spoon-fed on detailed printed instructions, this may seem like a great leap into the unknown, but in fact it holds the potential for greater adaptability of design to an individual's needs and opens up each pattern to the use of a wide range of yarns and threads. For example, design no. 27 is a nightgown yoke originally worked in a very fine cotton (equal to size 80 mercerised cotton). The design could still be used for that purpose and crocheted in the finest cotton, but by following the "work-to-measure" approach, this design could also be worked in a heavier weight thread or yarn and even extended to become a full-length blouse. The fact that it is worked in strips of small motifs makes such adaptation even easier. The potential variations for this and the other designs are endless.

It is hoped that with the accompanying hook and yarn charts, modern crocheters will be encouraged to experiment with these early crochet designs and experience the delight of creating their own unique crocheted fashions.

Gertrude Kuehl
January 1990

1

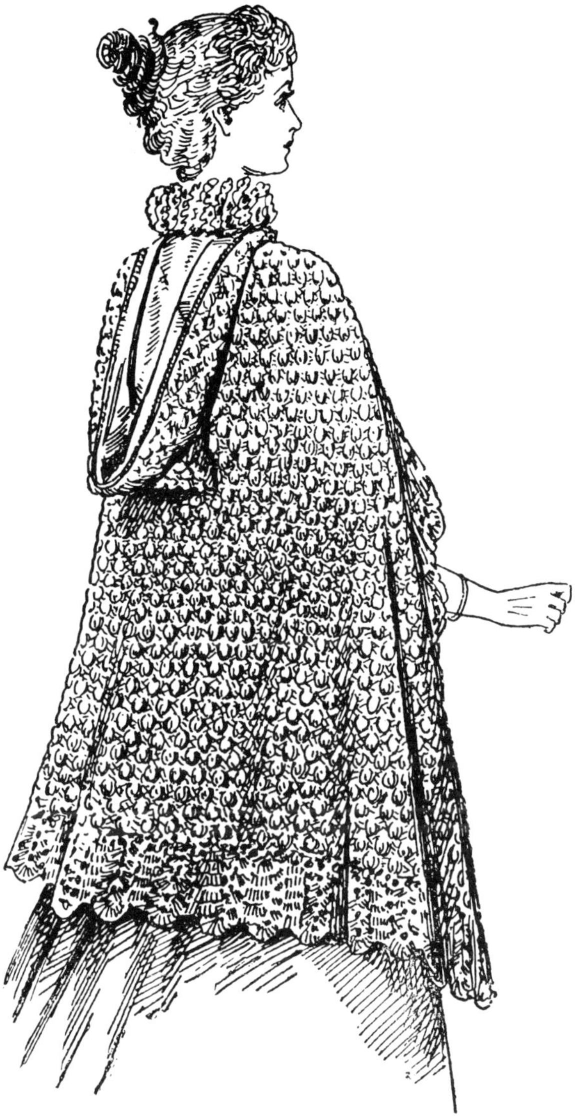

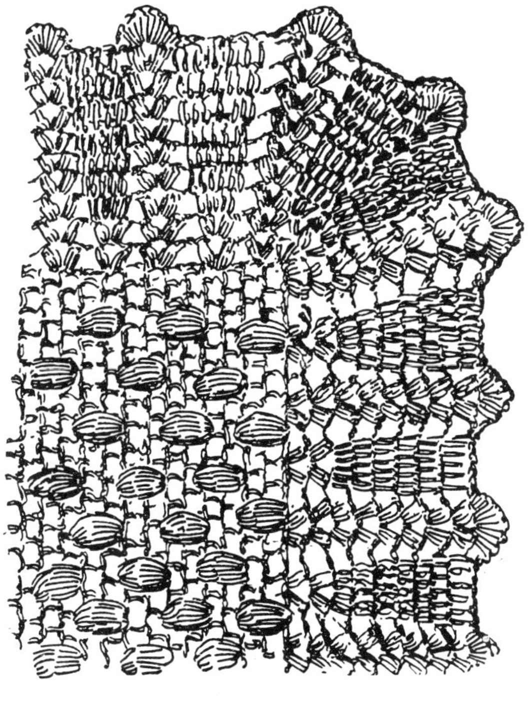

DETAIL OF WRAP.

WRAP FOR LADY, WITH HOOD.

This pretty as well as useful wrap is suitable for an invalid or evening wrap, as it is light, yet warm, and easily put on. Our model was made of 2-ply Camelaine undyed wool, but either 2-ply fingering, best quality, or Andalusian wool will make a nice wrap, and either of the last-named wools can be had in any colour wished, and would not be quite so expensive. Any sized wrap can be made by varying the number of stitches and rows. Our model measured when finished 68 inches in width and 34 in depth. Materials required for the above size:—13 ozs. of Camelaine undyed wool, 2 ivory or bone crochet hooks, Nos. 5 and 11, gauged by H. Walker's Patent Bell Gauge, $\frac{3}{4}$ of a yard of lining silk (to line the hood), a *chené* silk the colour of the wool shot with pink was used for model; $1\frac{1}{4}$ yard of silk cord to match the silk lining, and $\frac{5}{8}$ of a yard of $\frac{1}{2}$-inch white silk elastic. Commence at the bottom part of the wrap by working 168 chain with the No. 5 hook, allowing 4 chain for each pattern, work in rows, forwards and backwards, turning the work at the end of each row. 1*st row*—miss 1 chain stitch, and work 1 double crochet into each chain to the end of the row. Work 2 more rows of double crochet, working each stitch through both loops of each stitch of the previous row. 4*th row*—in this row the raised "tufts" are commenced. Work 3 double crochet stitches in the same way as in the two previous rows (working through both loops of the stitches) * for a "tuft," put the wool over the hook, insert the hook so as to take up the small *horizontal* thread of the 4 double crochet stitch in the 3rd preceding row, and draw the wool through loosely, wool over the hook and draw through 2 stitches or loops on the hook; make 6 more

(continued, p. 10)

(hooded wrap, continued from p. 9)

long loose stitches in the same way, wool again over the hook, and draw it through all the 8 loops on the hook, work a chain stitch to keep the "tuft" firm, miss the 1 double crochet stitch of the last row that is at the *back* of the "tuft," work 1 double in each of the next 3 stitches, and repeat from * to the end of the row. Work 3 rows of double crochet. 8*th row*—work 5 double crochet, then a "tuft" (as before in the 4th row). The "tufts" in this row should come between the "tufts" of the 4th row, ending the row with 5 double stitches to correspond with the beginning of the row. Work 3 rows of double crochet, and repeat from the 4th row till there are 17 patterns of light rows each worked.

For the Border.—The border is worked round three sides, leaving the top (or fourth side) for the neck, which is finished when the border is worked. 1*st row*—commence at the left-hand corner, and holding the right side (the side the "tufts" are on) towards you, * 2 treble into the next space, 2 chain, 2 treble in the same space as the last 2 treble were worked, miss the next space and repeat from * to the next corner; then work in the same way all along the bottom part of the wrap, making the 2 treble, 2 chain, 2 treble, into the foundation chain, and missing 3 stitches between the sets of 4 treble. Work the 3rd side to correspond with the 1st side. Fasten off the wool at the end of each row. 2*nd row*—2 treble, 2 chain, 2 treble, over the 2 chain of last row, repeat all along the 3 sides, and increasing at each of the 2 corners, so as to keep the work flat thus (2 treble, 2 chain, *three* times instead of twice. 3*rd row*—2 treble, 2 chain, 2 treble, over the first 2 chain, * 6 treble over the next 2 chain, 2 treble, 2 chain, 2 treble, over the next 2 chain, repeat from * to the corner, then work 6 treble over the next 2 chain, 2 chain, then repeat again from the first * to the next corner, which work to correspond with the first corner, and the third side the same as the first side. 4*th row*—2 treble, 2 chain, 2 treble, over the first 2 chain,* 1 treble into each of the 6 treble of the last row, working through both the loops of each stitch, 2 treble, 2 chain, 2 treble, over the next 2 chains; repeat from * to the corner, 6 treble into the next 6 treble, 2 treble, 2 chain, 2 treble over the next 2 chain, then repeat again from the first * to the second corner, which work to correspond with first corner, and the third side work as the first side. 5*th row*—the same as the 4th row, working at corners over the centre 2 chain. 6*th row*—the same as the 5th row, but over the centre; 2 chain at the corner, work 2 treble, 2 chain, 2 treble, 2 chain, 2 treble. 7*th row*—work to the corner the same as the last row, then over the first of the two corners, 3 chain, work 2 treble, 2 chain, 2 treble, over the next, 2 chain, 2 treble, 2 chain, 2 treble, and then work as last row to the second corner. Work it to correspond with the first corner, and finish the row the same way as the last row. 8*th row*—the same as the last row to the corner, then over the next 2 chain, work 2 treble, 2 chain, 2 treble, 1 treble, 2 chain, 1 treble between the next set of 4 treble, then over the next 2 chain, 2 treble, 2 chain, 2 treble. Continue the pattern as in last row, to the second corner, which work the same way as the first corner, and the third side same as the first side. 9*th row*—7 treble over the next 2 chains, * miss 3 treble stitches, 1 double crochet into each of the next 4 stitches, 3 treble, 3 long treble, (wool twice round the hook), 3 treble. All these 9 stitches are worked over the next 2 chains; repeat from * to corner, then work 2 sets of 9 stitches, same as the scallops already worked, with one double over the 2 chain between the two 1 treble stitches of the last row. Work the second side, second corner, and third side to correspond with the first corner and side already worked.

For the Neck.—Commence at the right-hand, having the right side of the wrap towards you. * 2 treble into the first space, 2 chain, miss 1 space; repeat from * all across the row. Fasten off the wool. 2*nd row*—over the first 2 chain, 2 treble, 3 long, 2 treble, * 1 double ever the next 2 chain, 2 treble, 2 chain, 2 treble over the next 2 chain; repeat from * all across the row. Fasten off the wool.

Case for the Elastic.—With the crochet hook No. 11 .make a chain the length of the elastic, which should be long enough to go easily round the neck, and work a row of 1 treble into each stitch, then on the opposite side of the foundation chain work a row the same as the first row. When the second row is worked, without breaking off the wool, place the elastic flat between the two rows, and work all along thus: Put the hook

(continued, p. 32)

SOVEREIGN PURSE.

NOTE: The sc in this pattern refers to the British double crochet; the symbol + is used to indicate repetition.

Materials.—1 skein of fine scarlet silk, 1 ditto white, 1 ditto black, 5 skeins of gold thread, No. 1, clasp with chain, and a few small round gold beads.

EACH side of this purse is done separately, and both precisely alike. With the gold thread make a chain of 4, close it into a round, and do two stitches in each.

2nd pattern Round.—2 Sc in every stitch.

3rd Round.—Gold and black. + 1 gold, 1 black, + 12 times in the round, increasing 8.

4th Round.—+ 2 gold on one, 1 black on black, + 12 times.

5th Round.—+ 3 gold over 2, 1 black on black, + 12 times.

6th Round.—Add white. + 1 gold, 1 white on 2nd gold, 1 gold, 1 black on black, + 12 times.

7th Round.—+ 1 gold and 1 white on gold, 1 white on white, 1 white and 1 gold on gold, 1 black on black, + 12 times.

8th Round.—+ 1 gold, 3 white, 1 gold, 1 black, + 12 times.

9th Round.—Add scarlet, and work one on the same stitch as the last black. + 1 black on gold, 1 gold, 1 white, 1 gold, 1 black, 1 scarlet, + 12 times. Fasten off white.

10th Round.—+ 2 scarlet, 1 black on gold, 1 gold on white, 1 black on gold, 1 more scarlet, + 12 times, working this round somewhat loosely. Fasten off the gold.

11th Round.—Do a black stitch on the gold of last round, and six scarlet between it and the next. Repeat this all round, and then fasten off the black, and do a round of scarlet only, increasing 12 stitches.

12th Round.—Scarlet, white and gold, + 3 scarlet, 2 gold, 2 white, 5 scarlet, 5 gold, 2 scarlet, + 6 times, thus increasing 3 in every pattern.

13th Round.—Join on black, + 5 scarlet (over 3 and 1 gold), 2 gold, 2 white, 4 scarlet (over 3 centre of 5), 2 gold 4 black on centre 3 gold, 2 gold, 1 scarlet, + 6 times.

14th Round.—+ 7 scarlet (over 5 and 1 gold), 2 gold, 2 white, 2 scarlet, 1 gold, 2 black, 5 scarlet over 4 black, 1 black, 2 gold, 1 black + 6 times.

15th Round.—+ 2 scarlet, 2 gold on one scarlet, 5 scarlet, 1 gold, 3 white, 1 gold on 2nd of 2 scarlet, 2 black, 6 scarlet, 1 black on black, 3 gold on 2, 1 black, + 6 times.

(continued, p. 12)

Crocheted Blouse for a Lady.

Abbreviations: ch., chain; d.c., double crochet; k., knit; p., purl.

THIS is a most comfortable garment for wearing at sports such as hockey, golf, etc., or for country or seaside wear. Use the best quality four-ply fingering, of which about 1¼ pounds will be necessary, and a No. 9 or No. 10 bone crochet hook, according to whether one crochets loosely or tightly. A pair of coarse steel knitting needles will also be required. The directions are for a medium-size garment.

Make 181 chain, miss the first chain by the hook, and work 180 short treble, as follows : wool over hook, insert the hook in a chain stitch, draw wool through, then wool over and draw through all three stitches on hook at once. This strip of crochet should measure from 29 inches to 30 inches, or long enough to reach from front waist-line over the shoulder to back waist.

2nd row—Loop stitch. Turn, 1 d.c. in first stitch, taking up both top

(continued, p. 12)

(blouse, continued from p. 11)

threads, draw the thread through next stitch, and from this loop work 4 ch., pull the final chain through the second stitch on hook ; repeat 1 d.c. and 1 loop stitch to end of row, where increase by working 2 d.c. in end stitch.

Work three rows of short treble, and increase one stitch at end of second of these rows. Work each stitch on the top back thread of the stitches of former row to give a ribbed effect.

These last four rows constitute the pattern, and in the model blouse each pattern of four rows measured an inch.

Work twenty rows, five patterns, for the width of the shoulder. The last row should end at front waist-line.

1st row of Front—Turn, and work 15 inches along the row, which brings the end of the new row up to the neck.

2nd row—Turn, miss first stitch, work to end, and there increase.

3rd row—In pattern, omitting the last stitch at neck.

Repeat the second and third rows until twenty-eight short rows are done, which should make the fronts wide enough to reach beyond the centre, double breasted, or if greater width is required it is easy enough to add one or even two more patterns, as required. Fasten off.

Return to the twentieth long shoulder row, and, commencing at the opposite end, work the first short row for centre of back. Count four stitches along from the end of the first front row, and begin there, working to waist-line of back. In each of the next three rows miss one stitch at top for shaping the neck, then work without increasing or decreasing until sixteen short rows are done. Work three more rows, increasing one stitch at top ; the last row ends at waist-line. Do not break off the wool, but leave the chain stitch for the present while you join on the wool at the upper end of this last row, and with it make sufficient chain to form a row equal in length to last long row of first shoulder. Fasten off.

Take up the chain loop which was left standing at opposite end, work along this row and right to the end of the chain ; this is the first long row for second shoulder. Work backwards and forwards until five patterns —twenty rows in all—are done, but *decrease* at the waist in the same manner as you increased for the opposite front. The last row of this second shoulder will end at the waist-line of the back. Fasten off. Go back to the chain added for the first row of this shoulder, and upon it work the short rows for the second front, beginning at waist, and shaping the neck as for first front.

The Under-arm Portions are now to be made. Commence at the front waist of the first foundation row. Work in pattern along 48 stitches of the chain, turn, and work to lower end again.

Work six more short rows, place the last row against the back foundation chain, and crochet them together. Work the other under-arm portion to correspond.

Now with the steel needles pick up all the stitches along the bottom of the blouse, and k. 1, p. 1 for about 2 inches, or deeper or shorter as may be required for the waistband. Cast off loosely.

For the Collar.—Crochet a row of short treble across the back from shoulder to shoulder. Crochet nine more rows in pattern, and increase one stitch at each end of each row.

For the Revers.—Crochet a row of short treble from one shoulder to end of front. Work fourteen more rows in pattern, here also increasing one stitch at each end of each row. Make a similar revers on the opposite front.

Finish all Edges with a tiny scallop as follows—1 d.c. into first stitch of a revers, 6 ch., slip-stitch into fourth chain from hook to form a picot, 2 ch., miss one stitch on revers, 1 d.c. in next ; repeat all round.

The Sleeves just turn the bend of the elbow.—Make a chain of 10½ inches.

Work four rows in pattern, increasing a stitch at the end of the last row.

5th row—Work to within 3½ inches of the end, turn, and work to top again.

7th row—Work to within 4½ inches of the bottom, turn, and work to top, where increase one stitch.

9th row—Work to within 6½ inches of the bottom, turn, and work to top.

11th row—Work from top to bottom, first along the tenth row, then along the ends of the various short rows, and lower portion of the fourth row.

Now along the entire length of this eleventh row work backwards and forwards for twenty rows, or until the sleeve is half wide enough, increasing one stitch at the top end of every second row for the first fourteen rows. When half the sleeve is thus made work back upon these directions for the second half, decreasing where you before increased, and *vice versa*.

Join the last row to foundation chain, to form the inner seam of the sleeve.

For the Cuff.—Begin at the centre of the back, and work one row round, but do not join. In working the cuff the right side must fall to the inside of the sleeve, so that when the cuff is rolled back the pattern will show on upper side.

2nd row—Turn, work in pattern, and increase one stitch at each end. Work twelve rows in all, backwards and forwards, increasing at each end of each row. Finish with a scallop edging to match the revers.

In sewing the sleeve in, gather any superfluous fulness over top of shoulder.

Fasten fronts in double-breasted effect, with pearl buttons, and button-holes made of chain loops or silk cord.

The stitch used for Crocheted Blouse—worked loosely to clearly show same.

(sovereign purse, continued from p. 10)

16th Round.— + 1 scarlet. 1 gold, 2 white, 1 gold, 4 scarlet, 1 gold, 2 white, 1 gold on gold, 1 black, 8 scarlet, 1 black on black, 3 gold on gold, 1 black, + 6 times.

17th Round.— + 2 scarlet, 1 gold, 1 white, 1 gold, 4 scarlet, 1 gold, 2 white, 2 gold, 4 white, 5 scarlet, 3 black on 3 gold, 1 scarlet, + 6 times.

18th Round.— + 2 scarlet, 1 gold, 1 white, 1 gold, 4 scarlet, 1 gold, 2 white, 6 gold, 2 white on 1 white, 1 scarlet, 8 scarlet, + 6 times.

19th Round.— + 3 scarlet, 1 gold, 1 white, 4 gold, 2 white, 4 gold, 3 black, 1 gold, 3 white, 5 scarlet, + 6 times.

20th Round.— + 4 scarlet, 1 gold, 4 white, 3 gold, 3 black, 5 scarlet, 2 white, 5 scarlet, + 6 times.

21st Round.— + 5 scarlet, 3 gold, 5 black, 8 scarlet, 1 white, 6 scarlet, + 6 times.

Finish each side with one round of scarlet only, and then crochet the two sides together, as far as the clasp leaves room.

For the edging, fasten on the gold thread, at the beginning of the joining, + 1 Dc, 1 Dc on same stitch, 3 Ch, Dc on same, Dc again on same. 1 Ch, miss 5, + repeat as far as the sides are joined.

Now do 9 Dc under each chain of 3, and 1 Sc under the 1 Ch, which completes the edging.

The neatest way to put on the clasp is to hold it over the edge of the silk, run the needle through a hole, thread a bead, and then return the needle though the same hole ; after which proceed to the next. This looks much prettier than the usual way of putting on a clasp, as no stitches are visible.

Crochet Wool Jacket.

Crochet Wool Jacket—Front.

Abbreviations : ch., chain ; tr., treble ; d.c., double crochet.

THIS jacket requires 5 ounces of single Berlin wool, with a bone hook to correspond. It is begun on the centre of the back at neck, and worked backwards and forwards over the shoulders from back to front.

Begin with 90 ch., 1 tr. into the third chain from the needle, 1 tr. into each of the next eleven chain. This forms the centre of the back. Leave the seventy-six chain in the meantime, and work another 76 ch.

1st row—3 ch., 1 tr. into the fourth chain from needle, 1 tr. into each of the next seventy-five chain, and 1 tr. into each of the twelve treble on the point at the back, 3 tr., 2 ch., 3 tr. over the three chain on the point, 1 tr. into each of the twelve treble up the other side of the point, 1 tr. into each of the seventy-six chain first worked, 2 ch., 3 tr. into the same stitch as last treble.

2nd row—3 ch., 1 tr. into each of the first three treble, 1 tr. into the first of the two chain between treble, 2 ch., 1 tr. into the second of the two chain, 1 tr. into each treble up one side till the point on the back is reached, 3 tr., 2 ch., 3 tr. over the two chain between treble, 1 tr. into each treble down the other side to the end of the row, 2 ch., 3 tr. over the three chain at the end of row. (Take the back thread of the stitch all through the work to give it a ribbed effect.) The edge of the front of the jacket is worked along with the rows.

3rd row—3 ch., 1 tr. into each of the first three treble, 1 tr. into the

Back View.

(continued, p. 14)

(continued from p. 13)

first of the two chain between treble, 2 ch., 1 tr. into the second of two chain, 1 tr. into each treble up one side till the point on the back is reached, 3 tr., 2 ch., 3 tr. over the two chain between treble, 1 tr. into each treble down the other side to the end of the row, 3 tr., 2 ch., 3 tr. over the space of two chain between treble.

4th row—* 3 ch., 1 tr. into each of the first three treble, 1 tr. into the first of the two chain between treble, 2 ch., 1 tr. into the second of the two chain, 1 tr. into each treble up one side till the point on the back is reached, 3 tr., 2 ch., 3 tr. over the two chain between treble, 1 tr. into each treble down the other side to the end of the row, 3 tr., 2 ch., 3 tr. over the space of two chain between treble.

5th row—3 ch., 1 tr. into each of the first three treble, 1 tr. into the first of the two chain between treble, 2 ch., 1 tr. into the second of two chain, 1 tr. into each treble up one side till the point on the back is reached, 3 tr., 2 ch., 3 tr. over the two chain between treble on the point, 1 tr. into each treble down the other side to the end of row, 3 tr., 2 ch., 3 tr. over the space of two chain between treble.

Work the fourth and fifth rows alternately, increasing on the beginning and end of each row till there are seventeen rows on the work. Do the eighteenth row as far as the last treble before two chain on the point on the back, then turn, and do 3 ch., 1 tr. into each treble along the side just worked, increasing on the end of the row. Work the rows backwards and forwards from the point on the back to the front of the jacket for seven rows. At the end of the seventh row begin the under-arm. Turn, 3 ch., 1 tr. into each of the next thirty-six treble. Turn, 3 ch., 1 tr., 1 tr. into each of the next thirty-six treble. Turn, 1 tr. into each of the next thirty-six treble. Finish off the wool. Work three other rows on the front of the jacket to complete the under-arm, join the wool to the sixty-first treble from the two chain on the point on the front of the jacket, leaving twenty-five free treble from the point, 3 ch., 1 tr. into each of the next thirty-six treble. Turn, 3 ch., 1 tr. into each of the next thirty-six treble. Turn, 3 ch., 1 tr. into each of the next thirty-six treble. Join the front under-arm to the back under-arm (do not break off the wool), 1 ch., draw the wool through the first treble on the back part of under-arm, then through the stitch on the needle (this makes two chain), 1 ch., miss two treble on the front part, * draw the wool through the stitch on the needle, again making two chain, 1 ch., miss two treble on the next side and repeat from * till both sides of the under-arm are joined. Finish off the wool firmly. In working the second side of the coat join the wool to the first treble on the other side of the point on the back, and work backwards and forwards for seven rows as directed for first side. Instead of beginning the second under-arm, on the back of jacket, from the end of the row as done on the first side, begin on the thirty-sixth treble from the end of the row, and work down. Do the front under-arm, and join in the same way as directed for the first side.

The Edge.—Join the wool to the first treble on the neck, 3 ch. for treble, 1 tr. into same stitch, 2 ch., 2 tr. into same stitch, miss three treble, 2 tr., 2 ch., 2 tr. into next stitch, * miss three treble, 2 tr., 2 ch., 2 tr. into next stitch. Repeat from * all round the neck and arm-holes. Join the wool to the first treble on the point of the jacket.

1st row—3 ch. for treble, 1 tr., 2 ch., 2 tr. into the same stitch, * miss three treble, 2 tr., 2 ch., 2 tr. into the same stitch; repeat from * from one point on front along the back of the jacket to second point on front.

2nd row—Turn, 3 ch., 2 tr., 3 ch., 3 tr. over the first space of two chain between treble, * 3 tr., 3 ch., 3 tr. over the next space between treble; repeat from * along the back of the jacket to the second front. Work one row of picots down the two fronts of the jacket. Join the wool to the treble where the last treble on neck was worked, * slip-stitch into the top of the first treble on front edge, 3 ch., slip-stitch into the same stitch, slip-stitch to the top of next treble, 3 ch., slip-stitch into the same stitch, slip-stitch over the next treble, 3 ch., slip-stitch into the same stitch, slip-stitch into the large space between six treble; repeat from * down both sides of the front of the jacket.

To make the button. Make a small ring of the wool, leaving one end free, with a small bone hook work over this ring 5 d.c., and draw the five double crochet tightly together with the end left free. Work round and round the ring, increasing every second stitch, till there is sufficient to cover a button. Take a needle and draw all the stitches together into a little bag; put either a button or some cotton-wool into it, and draw together. Sew it on to the jacket. Work a few chain, and sew on the jacket for a loop.

✼✼✼

Crochet Flowers

FUCHSIA.

Red Star Sylko No. 5, for petals; Purple Star Sylko No. 5, for cup; Green Star Sylko No. 5, for leaves.

STRANDS.—Wind the red silk round a piece of cardboard, 3 inches wide about 7 or 8 times. Slip it off and tie about ¼ inch from one end. Tie again ¾ inch from the last tie. Cut through the loops at the other end and trim off the edges.

PURPLE CUP.—5 ch., join into ring, 12 d.c. into ring. 5 rows of d.c., 1 in each stitch and fasten off. Draw the red strands through the hole in the cup leaving loose ends hanging below the cup.

RED PETALS.—Wind silk 3 times round end of lead pencil, slip off. Draw a loop of silk through the ring with the hook, and secure with 1 ch. * Make 9 ch., miss 1, 1 d.c. in each of 2 ch., 1 tr. in each of 2 ch., 1 l.tr. (cotton twice over hook), in each of 4 ch., catch down, into ring with sl. st. Repeat from * 3 times more. Slip the ring of petals over the red strands to fit on the top of purple cup, secure it in place with a few stitches.

GREEN STEMS.—Take a long strand of green silk, double it, put the hook through the tied end of the red strands, and pull the double end of green silk through. Now work ch. with the double strands for about 5 inches. Fasten off. Join on to middle of green stem, make 9 ch. and work a green leaf like one of the red petals, catch down to the ch. where the leaf started.

Work a second flower and stem, putting 2 green leaves on the stem to vary it.

Star Stitch Camisole.

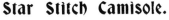

Abbreviations : ch., chain ; tr., treble ; d.c., double crochet.

MATERIALS : 4 to 6 ounces of J. & J. Baldwin's Beehive **Lady** Betty fleecy wool and a No. 0 steel crochet hook.

Our model is worked for a 36-inch bust measurement, but this camisole can be made any size desired by getting the correct length for the first chain, that is, from the waistline at the back, over the shoulder, and down to the waistline in front, and working across the back and fronts according to the width of figure.

Make the length of chain desired, and work in star stitch as follows : Miss the first chain, take up a loop in each of the first four chains (to take up a loop simply insert the hook in the chain stitch and draw wool through), wool over hook and draw through the five loops now on the hook, make 1 ch. to form the eye, and the star is complete. * Draw the wool through the eye of the previous star to make a loop, also a loop through the back of last loop of first star, and through the next two chain stitches ; thus you get five loops on hook, wool over hook, draw through all five loops, make 1 ch. to form eye ; repeat from * to the end of the row.

2nd row—Turn with 3 ch., miss the first chain, take up a loop in the next two chain, one loop in the eye of the first star on previous row, one loop in the back of first loop of same star, draw through the five loops, and make 1 ch. as usual ; * 3 ch., pick up a loop in the last two chain, a loop in the eye of the next star on previous row, and a loop in the first loop at the back of same star, and repeat from * to the end of the row.

Work two more rows like second row, the fourth row ending at the front waistline.

5th row—Increase one star at the beginning of this row by making a star in the end of previous row, then work stars until the row is 9 inches long, or until the top edge of the left front is reached according to whether the camisole is wanted high or low at the neck. Work backwards and forwards in star stitch on this short row until thirty-four rows in all are completed, increasing one star at the beginning of every fourth row, but, as all figures vary, measure the work and see if it is wide enough for half a front before fastening off ; if not, as many rows of star stitch may be added as are required.

Now return to the last long row of the shoulder, which is the last row before the short row was commenced for the left front. From the end of this short row count along twenty-five stars, or more or less according

(continued, p. 16)

LADIES' RIBBED CROCHET TIE,
WITH SHAPED ENDS.

Crochet Tie, with shaped ends To be worked in Briggs' crochet silk or Silver Shield crochet thread.

Work 13 chain and 1 to turn.

1st row — 13 double crochet.

2nd row-1 double crochet into each stitch of previous row worked into the back thread only.

3rd and following rows, the same as 2nd until 9 inches are worked. Then for the shaped end, work.

1st row--1 double crochet into each of first six stitches of previous row, 3 double crochet into the 7th or middle stitch of the row, 1 double crochet into each of the next 6 stitches.

2nd row—1 double crochet in each stitch of previous row until the middle stitch is reached, 3 double crochet into middle stitch, and 1 double crochet into each of remaining stitches, except the last stitch, which is left unworked.

3rd and following rows are worked in the same way, namely increasing by 3 double crochet into each middle stitch and leaving the last stitch of each row unworked.

Work for 32 ridges or more if required longer.

This completes one half the tie, the other half is worked in the same way and neatly joined at centre of neckband.

The fringe should be crocheted on over a piece of card about 2 inches deep. Cut the edges and divide the strands at the top by clustering into groups, and knotting with a needle and thread as for drawn thread work.

The tie is improved in shape if the ends are kept well pulled in ironing.

(camisole, continued from p. 15)

to the height you wish the neck at the back to be ; if the neck is wanted high, leave less stars unworked, and if low, more stars. In the twenty-sixth star begin to work, and continue to lower edge. This is the first short row of the back ; on it work twenty-seven rows in all, or as many rows as are required to bring the work to the second shoulder, the last row ending at the top. At the end of this row make a chain long enough to give a total length when added to the last row to equal the length of the long shoulder rows on the other side. Turn, work along the chain and along the row down to the back waistline, which makes the first long shoulder row for this side. Work three more rows in star stitch, and fasten off.

Go back to the chain added for the first long shoulder row, and count twenty-five stars from the first short row of the back, or as many stars as required to start the right front on a level with the first front according to whether the neck is made high or low, and work as instructed from the fifth row of the left front, but increasing the star at the end of the fifth row so that it will be at the waistline. Fasten off.

Sew up the underarm seams, leaving enough unjoined at the top for the armhole. Round the waist work nine rows of double crochet, decreasing on each front (to bring the belt to the right size) by missing a stitch here and there, according to size of waist. Make a buttonhole at the right hand side of the belt in the fourth row by missing two double crochet and making two chain instead ; then in the fifth row put 1 d.c. in each of the two chain.

Around the armholes work eight rounds of double crochet, commencing at the underarm seam, and at that point decrease one stitch in each round. Before starting a new round always turn the work to give the same effect as on the waistbelt. Make a fancy edge round the sleeve in the final round as follows : 1 d.c. in the first stitch, * 1 ch., 2 tr. in the same stitch, 3 ch., slip-stitch to top of last treble worked to form a picot, miss three double crochet, 1 d.c. in the next stitch, and repeat from * all round the armhole, and fasten off.

To make the square neck work thirteen rows of double crochet, on the first round gathering in the fulness of the fronts by missing a stitch here and there according to the size required, and on the second and the following rows miss two stitches at each corner to make the square neck. Make a fancy edge as on armholes, and fasten off. Work a buttonhole on the right hand side of the band as instructed for the waistbelt. Stitch five buttons on the left front, as shown in the illustration, but for the three centre buttonholes simply buttonhole-stitch with silk round one of the spaces between the stars.

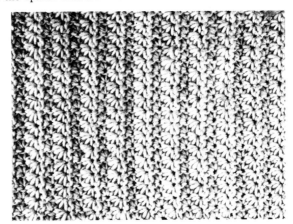

Example of several rows of completed star stitch crochet

COLLAR.—MIGNONNETTE.

Taylor's Crochet Thread, No. 10; Needle, No. 22, Bell Gauge.—Make a chain of 265 stitches, and work backwards and forwards

1st row.—5 chain, miss 2, 1 plain, repeat, and end with 2 plain.

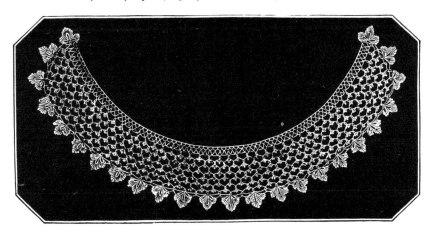

2d.—5 chain, miss 5, 1 plain in the 5 chain of 1st row : repeat.

3d.—5 chain, miss 3, 1 plain, *, (7 chain, 1 plain in the 2nd chain stitch, to form a round loop,) 1 chain, miss 5, 1 plain in the 5 chain of last row, 5 chain, miss 5, 1 plain in the 5 chain of last row : repeat from *, and end with 1 plain.

4th.—5 chain, miss 9, *, (1 plain, and 3 chain 3 times, 1 plain, these four plain stitches are all to be worked in the round loop of the 3rd row ;) 7 chain, 1 plain in the 2nd chain stitch, to form a round loop, 1 chain, miss 7, repeat from *, and end with (1 plain, and 3 chain 3 times,) 1 plain in the round loop as before, 2 chain, miss 3, 1 plain in the 5 chain.

5th.—5 chain, miss 17, *, (1 plain, and 3 chain 3 times, 1 plain, these 4 plain are to be worked in the round loop of 4th row,) 11 chain, 1 plain in the 3rd chain stitch, to form a round loop, 2 chain, miss 17, repeat from *, end with 1 plain, and 3 chain 3 times, 1 plain, the plain stitches in the round loop as before, 2 chain, miss 7, 1 plain in the centre loop of the 4th row.

6th.—5 chain, miss 17 *, (1 plain, and 4 chain 4 times, 1 plain, these 5 plain stitches are to be worked in the round loop, of 5th row,) 11 chain, 1 plain in the 3d chain stitch, to form a round loop, 2 chain, miss 17, repeat from *, end with 1 plain, and four chain 4 times, 1 plain, the plain stitches are worked as before, 2 chain, miss 7, 1 plain in loop of the 5th row.

7th and 8th.—The same ; missing 25 instead of 17, and, at the end of the 8th row, cut off the thread and fasten it.

9th—Commence at the foundation and work up the side, thus :—11 chain, 1 plain in the 3d stitch, to form a loop as before, 2 chain, 1 plain in the chain at the side, repeat 5 times, 11 chain, 1 plain, the 3rd stitch as before, 2 chain, and repeat from the * in the 6th row, missing 25 instead of 17, as before, at the end, work 6 round loops down the side as at the commencement of this row.

(continued, p. 18)

SECTION OF COLLAR.

(collar, continued from p. 17)

10th.—3 chain, miss 3, 7 plain in the round loop, of the 9th row,*, 3 chain, miss 5, (1 plain, 9 chain, 1 plain, 11 chain, 1 plain, 9 chain, 1 plain ; these 4 plain are worked in the next round loop of the 9th row,) 3 chain, miss 5, 7 plain in the next round loop, repeat from * once more, for the side, and work the same along the 9th row, missing 24 instead of 5 stitches.

11th.—(1 plain, and 4 chain, 6 times, 1 plain ; these 7 plain stitches are to be worked in the 9 chain of last row) miss 3, (1 plain and 4 chain, 9 times, 1 plain ; these 10 plain stitches are worked in the 11 chain of last row) miss 3, (1 plain, and four chain, 6 times, 1 plain ; these 7 plain stitches in the 9 chain of last row), 2 chain, miss 6, 1 plain on the centre of the 7 plain in last row, 2 chain, miss 6, repeat, end with 1 plain. and fasten off.

TULIP.

Yellow Star Sylko No. .5, for tulip ; Red Star Sylko No. 5, for markings ; Green Star Sylko No. 5, for leaf.

FLOWER.—Follow the instructions for narcissus petal, but work 5 rows to make petals a little larger. Work 4 petals. Thread a needle with the red silk and work lines in each petal to represent markings. Take two petals, double the ends, and insert one inside the other. Put two or three stitches in to keep in place. Take the other two petals and place round the inside two, stitch at the bottom. Take the green silk, and make a stem of several strands at the bottom of flower.

LEAF.—Follow instructions for the narcissus leaf, but work an extra round working treble each side in the middle of leaf to increase the width. Stitch the flower to the leaf a little way from the bottom.

Any of these flowers can be carried out in wool with just the same effect. Use 3-ply wool and then the size will be about the same.

Rose Scent Sachet in Crochet.

Abbreviations : ch., chain ; tr., treble ; d.c., double crochet : l.t., long treble.

MATERIALS : Three balls of D.M.C. Coton Perlé No. 8 (two shades of pink, one of green), a No. 4 steel crochet hook, a small piece of pink muslin or silk, and some rose scent powder.

Make a sachet of silk, about 3½ inches long, slightly pointed at each end, measuring about 3¼ inches round the middle. Fill with powder.

Make seven petals—one small, three medium, three large.

For Small Petal.—Commence with 7 ch. Join in a ring, into which work 12 l.t. (cotton twice over needle). Turn.

2nd row—* 4 ch. to represent one long treble, 1 l.t. on long treble, 2 l.t. into next stitch, and repeat from * to end of row, taking up both loops of stitch in each row except the last, turn.

3rd row—3 ch., 1 tr. into each long treble, increasing one in every third stitch. Turn.

4th row—3 ch., 1 tr. in each stitch. No increasing.

5th row—3 ch., 1 l.t. into each of first three treble (taking up back loop only), 1 tr. into rest of row. Fasten off.

Medium Petals.—Commence with 8 ch. Join into a ring, into which work 16 l.t.

Work five rows of long treble as in small petal, increasing one in every second stitch, then one round of treble, plain (no increasing).

8th row—1 d.c. into each of first three treble, 1 tr. into each treble, putting a few long treble in centre of petal to shape it, then 1 tr. into each treble until the last three are reached, where work a double crochet to each.

9th row—As eighth row, but being the last row, only take up the back loop of each stitch.

Work one petal entirely in the paler shade of cotton, and two in the paler with last two or three rows in darker shade.

Large Petals.—Work two large petals in darker shade, and one in half light and half dark.

Commence with 8 ch., join into ring, into which work 19 l.t. Work six rows of long treble, then work last two rows as in medium petals.

Join these petals over one half of silk case, covering the top with a medium petal in light colour, and arrange small petals next, and the rest to represent a rose. Tack in place.

For the lower part of sachet a green covering is required.

Commence with 3 ch., join in ring, into which work 15 l.t. ; join the last to first with a slip-stitch.

2nd round—4 ch., * 1 l.t. into first long treble, 2 l.t. in next, and repeat from * all round. Join.

3rd round—4 ch., 1 l.t. in each stitch (no increasing).

4th round—Same as third round.

5th round—Same as third round.

6th round—Same as third round.

Count the stitches, and divide into four. In each quarter work 2 d.c., 3 tr., 2 l.t., 1 triple treble (cotton three times over hook), 2 l.t., 3 tr., 2 d.c., and fasten off.

For the Stalk.—Join cotton to lower end, and work 30 ch., and into each work 1 d.c. Fasten off ; place the green case over lower half of sachet, tack in place, and the sachet is finished.

The Rose "Peter Pan" Collar.

Abbreviations : ch., chain ; tr., treble ; s.c., single crochet ; d.c., double crochet.

MATERIALS required : White or cream D.M.C. Coton Perlé, size 8, or Ardern's crochet cotton No. 20, and a steel crochet hook, size 4.

Seven roses are required for the collar, each worked separately.

For a Rose.—8 ch., join in a ring with single crochet.

1st row—6 ch. (three to stand for a treble), 1 tr. into the ring, * 3 ch., 1 tr. into the ring ; repeat from * six times more, 3 ch., 1 s.c. into the third chain of the six first worked. There must be nine holes round the ring.

2nd row—Into each hole work 1 d.c., 5 tr., 1 d.c.

3rd row—9 ch. (three to stand for a treble), 1 tr. into the first treble of first row, turning the petal of previous row forward, so that the stitch can be easily picked up ; * 6 ch., 1 tr. in the next treble at the back of the petal, as just described, and repeat from * all round, finishing with 6 ch., and working 1 s.c. into the third chain of the nine first worked.

4th row—Into each hole work 1 d.c., 8 tr., 1 d.c.

5th row—11 ch. (three to stand for a treble), 1 tr. into the first treble of third row, working at the back of petal of previous row, * 8 ch., 1 tr. into next treble, and repeat from *, finishing with 8 ch., and joining with a single crochet to the third chain of the eleven first worked.

6th row—Into each hole work 1 d.c., 10 tr., 1 d.c.

7th row—1 s.c. into the first three stitches of the first petal, * 8 ch., 1 s.c. into the fifth chain from the hook, to form a picot ; 8 ch., 1 s.c. into the third chain from the hook, 3 ch., miss six treble on the same petal, 1 d.c. into next treble, 8 ch., picot, 8 ch., picot, 3 ch., 1 d.c. on the second treble on next petal, and repeat from * all round.

8th row—Slip-stitch along the chain to the centre between two picots, * 8 ch., picot, 8 ch., picot, 3 ch., 1 d.c. between next two picots of previous row, and repeat from * all round. Finish off, and work six more roses, joining each successive rose to the previous one at the centre of three consecutive double picots, leaving always seven picots along one side of the roses, and five along the other. Along the side where there are five double picot loops on the roses join the cotton to centre of the fourth double picot on the first rose, counting from the junction of the two roses. Work 2 ch., 1 tr. in the same place, 3 ch., 3 tr., all in the same place between the two picots, * 7 ch., 3 d.c. between the next two picots, 7 ch., 3 tr. between next two picots, 18 ch., 1 s.c. into the fifth chain from the hook (to form a picot), 3 ch., 1 d.c. between next two picots, 1 picot, 3 ch., 1 d.c. into the double crochet which joins the picots of the roses together ; 1 picot, 3 ch., 1 d.c. between first two picots on next rose ; 1 picot, 3 ch. Turn the work and put 1 s.c. into the second chain above the picot which was worked on long chain on previous rose ; 3 ch., miss three chain of this same long chain, 1 s.c. into next chain, 7 ch. Turn, 3 tr. between next double picot on second rose, and repeat from * all along, finishing with 3 tr., 3 ch., 2 tr. into the last space, to correspond with the first side of the collar.

(continued, p. 20)

(rose collar, continued from p. 19)

Pass down the end of the collar, working 3 ch., 1 tr. on to the double crochet between the first two double picots, * 5 ch., 1 d.c. under the chain between the picots, 5 ch. 1 tr. on the next double crochet between the picots of previous round, and continue all round the rose until the last double picot is reached. Work 1 d.c. between the two picots, 4 ch., 1 d.c. after the left-hand picot, 4 ch., 1 d.c. on to the double crochet which joins the roses, 4 ch., 1 d.c. before the first picot of the next double picot ; 4 ch., 1 d.c. between the picots and work round the scallop, as described for the first one.

When the end of collar is reached, join up the row with a single crochet into the chain which was worked after joining on the cotton, and work 3 d.c. into the first space (before three treble stitches), 4 ch., 1 tr. on the first treble of the three, 2 ch., * 1 tr. on the last treble of the same group ; 2 ch., 1 tr. into the fourth chain of the seven ; 2 ch., 1 tr. on the first double crochet, 2 ch., 1 tr. on the last double crochet of the same group ; 2 ch., 1 tr. into the fourth chain, 2 ch., 1 tr. on the next treble, 2 ch., 1 tr. on the last treble of same group ; 2 ch., miss one chain, 1 tr. in next chain, 2 ch., miss two, 1 tr. in next, 2 ch., 1 tr. under the stitch which joined the long chain ; 2 ch., miss two, 1 tr. in next, 2 ch., miss two, 1 tr. in next, 2 ch., 1 tr. in first treble of the group of three now reached, 2 ch., and repeat from * all along.

Work double crochet down the end of the row closely until the first loop of chain is reached ; here work 3 d.c., 3 ch., 3 d.c. into this loop, 2 d.c. into next loop, 4 ch. Turn, 1 s.c. into the third double crochet from the hook. Turn, and fill the loop just made with 3 d.c., 3 ch., 3 d.c., 2 d.c. into the same loop on the edge again, 3 ch., 2 d.c. in the same loop ; * pass over the double crochet to the next loop, and work 3 d.c., 3 ch., 3 d.c., 2 d.c. into next loop, 4 ch. Turn, 1 s.c. into the third double crochet from the hook, fill the loop just made with 3 d.c., 3 ch., 3 d.c., 2 d.c. into same loop on edge, again 3 ch., 2 d.c. in the same loop, and repeat from * all round, omitting one small loop at either side of the junction of the roses.

Work double crochet up the end of the row at neck, 3 ch., 2 tr. in the first space, * 2 ch., miss one space, 3 tr. in next, and repeat from * all along, 2 ch. Turn, 1 tr. on the first treble, 1 rather loose chain, * 1 tr. on the last treble of the same group, 1 ch. (always rather loosely worked), 1 tr. on next tr., 1 ch., and repeat from * all along, 1 ch. Turn and work 1 d.c. into first space, 5 ch., 1 s.c. into first chain to form a picot, another d.c. in same space, 1 d.c. in next space, 2 d.c. in next space, 1 d.c. in next space, 5 ch., picot, and continue working 1 d.c. and 2 d.c. alternately into every space, making a picot on every fifth stitch.

Button

For *this Button* get a wooden mould about half-an-inch in diameter, and work the cover for it as follows, in rabbit wool (see sketch) :—3 ch., secure into a ring by means of 1 single crochet stitch, then 2 double crochet on each ch. of ring, and continue to work in the same way, taking up only the back thread of each stitch to form a rib.

The Button

1st to *3rd row.*—Alternately 2 d.c. on the d.c., 1 d.c. on the next d.c.

4th and *5th rows.*—1 d.c. on each d.c. of previous row.

Now finish with a few rows of intakes to draw it in to fit the mould, by passing over one stitch in every third one of the row.

Crochet with Metallic Threads

ALL kinds of dress accessories are being formed for evening wear from the metallic and tinsel threads to meet the great demand for this kind of work at present so much the vogue.

This is one of the very easiest forms of crochet, and one that gives best results from very little work. Silver and gold threads are used for the more expensive articles, but for trimming an evening frock, and making ornamental bands, belts, girdles, etc., the tinsel thread, sold in penny balls, gives very charming effects at little cost.

A COLLAR IN TINSEL SILVER THREAD FOR EVENING WEAR.—Using a No. 1 steel crochet hook, or a fine bone one, and working rather loosely, make a length of chain stitches sufficient to go round the neck of the blouse or bodice, 3 ch., * 3 tr. into 4 ch. of foundation, 3 ch., 1 d.c. into next fourth ch., 3 ch. Repeat from *, end the row as at the beginning.

2nd row.—7 ch. 1 d.c. into each loop.

3rd row.—* 3 ch. 1 d.c. into first loop, 3 ch. 1 d.c. into next d.c. * Repeat into each loop.

4th row.—7 ch. 1 d.c. into each d.c. on centre of preceding loops.

5th row.—Same as the *3rd* from which * you repeat until four rows of double loops are completed, then finish the collar with 10 ch. 1 d.c. into every d.c. in last row.

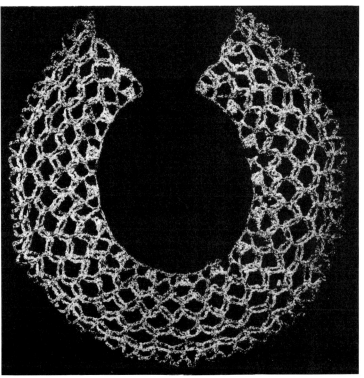

Collar in Silver Tinsel

Butterfly Ornament.

Abbreviations : ch., chain ; tr., treble ; d.c., double crochet.

MATERIALS : Three 4½d. reels of Head's silver (or gold) thread No. 5, and a steel crochet hook size 4 ; also a reel of flower wire will be required, a few inches of millinery wire, a scrap of buckram, and a small piece of cotton wool. This could also be used as an ornament for the front of an evening dress, with a safety-pin sewn on the back for attachment.

Commence the large wings of the butterfly with 12 chain.

1st row—Miss five chain, 1 treble into next, * 2 ch., miss one chain, 1 tr. into next ; repeat from * twice more, 5 ch., turn.

2nd row—1 d.c. into first space, * 5 ch., 1 d.c. into next space ; repeat from * to end of row, 5 ch., turn.

3rd row—1 d.c. into first space, * 5 ch., 1 d.c. into next space ; repeat from * to end of row, 5 ch., 1 d.c. in last space again, 5 ch., turn.

4th row—1 d.c. into first space, 5 ch., 1 d.c. into next space, 2 ch., 5 tr. into next space, 2 ch., 5 tr. into next space, 2 ch., 1 d.c. into next space, 5 ch., 1 d.c. into next space, 5 ch., 1 d.c. into last space again, 5 ch., turn.

5th row—1 d.c. into first space, 5 ch., 1 d.c. into same space, 5 ch., 1 d.c. into next space, 5 ch., 1 d.c. into next space, 5 ch., 1 d.c. into the centre treble of the group, * 5 ch., 1 d.c. into next space ; repeat from * to end of row, 5 ch., turn.

6th row—1 d.c. into first space, 5 ch., 1 d.c. into next space, 5 ch., 5 tr. into next space, 2 ch., 5 tr. into next space, * 5 ch., 1 d.c. into next space, and repeat from * to end of row, 5 ch., 1 d.c. into last space again, 5 ch., turn.

7th row—1 d.c. into first space, * 5 ch., 1 d.c. into next space ; repeat from * to end of row, working into the space of two chain between the groups of treble, 5 ch., 1 d.c. into same space again, 5 ch., turn.

8th row—1 d.c. into first space, * 5 ch., 1 d.c. into next space ; repeat from * to end of row, 5 ch., turn. There should be nine spaces across the lace. Work two more rows like the eighth row, and fasten off.

Take the flower wire, cut off a length of 30 inches, bend this into three, making the piece 10 inches long. Lay this treble strand of wire along the edge of the wing just made, and work double crochet over it into the holes down the side of the wing, filling the holes and working a loop of 4 ch. at every fifth stitch. Work three loops of 4 ch. at the corner hole, and 3 d.c., 4 ch., 3 d.c. into each hole along the top of the wing. Continue down second side as for first and fasten off.

Make a second large wing.

For the small wings commence with 8 chain.

1st row—1 tr. into fifth chain from hook, 2 ch., 1 tr. into last chain, 5 ch., turn.

2nd row—1 d.c. into first space, 5 ch., 1 d.c. into same space, 5 ch., 1 d.c. into next space, 5 ch., turn.

3rd row—1 d.c. into first space, 5 ch., 1 d.c. into same space, 5 ch. and 1 d.c. into each remaining space, 5 ch., turn.

4th row—Same as third row, 5 ch., turn.

5th row—1 d.c. into first space, 5 ch., 1 d.c. into each remaining space, 5 ch., turn.

Work four more rows like the fifth row.

Surround the small wing with wire in the same manner as the large wing. Work a second small wing.

For the body commence with 3 chain.

1st row—3 d.c. into second chain, 1 ch., turn.

2nd row—1 d.c. into first double crochet, 1 d.c. into second double crochet, 2 d.c. into last double crochet, 1 ch., turn.

Repeat the second row eight times, when there should be twelve stitches across.

Work fourteen rows backwards and forwards without increasing the number of stitches, always turning with 1 ch.

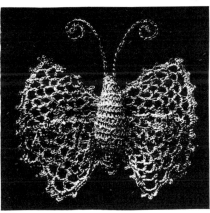

Butterfly ornament for the hair, dress, or hat. (*See page 6.*)

25th row—Miss one double crochet, 1 d.c. into each of the remaining stitches except the last stitch, 1 d.c. turn. Do two rows of 1 d.c. into every stitch. Repeat the last three rows until only four stitches remain, and fasten off.

For the antennæ cut a piece of wire 16 inches, double it, then double in half again, insert the hook into the last loop formed, and draw cotton through ; work 1 d.c. into loop. Then, working over all four strands of wire at once, work 35 d.c. along it. Fasten off.

Spread the stitches down the wire to conceal it, and curl the top round as naturally as possible. Take the buckram and cut a narrow piece about 2 inches long and ¾ inch wide, pointed at each end. Sew millinery wire round it. Attach the two large wings, then the two small.

Form a small piece of cotton wool into a roll 2½ inches long, thick at middle and pointed at ends. Stretch the crochet body section over this, pressing into a nice shape. Sew the antennæ to the buckram at the top between the large wings, and finally sew the body firmly on to the buckram. Arrange the wings as naturally as possible, and sew a firm hairpin at back.

Crocheted Buckle. 15

Buckle for a belt or hat.

Abbreviations : ch., chain ;

tr., treble ; d.c., double crochet.

SUITABLE for waist-band, millinery purposes, etc.

Materials : Ardern's Star Sylko No. 3 and No. 8, with a No. 4½ steel crochet hook and a darning-needle to take the No. 3 Sylko.

An old metal buckle can be used or the shape cut in thick cardboard, not forgetting to leave a bar across the centre over which the ribbon passes.

First cover the buckle or shape with material to match the colour of the thread to be used ; the material should be cut in narrow strips and bound evenly round, finally securing it with a few strong stitches.

Now take the No. 3 Sylko, and, beginning at the top left-hand corner, make button-hole stitches closely together over the buckle and the centre bar and fasten off.

For the edging use the No. 4½ hook and the No. 8 Star Sylko, and begin at the top right-hand corner, put 1 d.c. in each of the first seven stitches, passing the hook under the pearl edge of the button-holing, 5 ch., slip-stitch into the first chain to form a picot, 1 d.c. in each of the next four stitches, * 12 ch., turn the work and put a double crochet in the fourth of the seven double crochet worked before the picot, 4 d.c. in the loop of twelve chain, 5 ch. to form a picot, 4 d.c., picot, 4 d.c., picot, 4 d.c. all in the loop of twelve chain, 3 d.c. along the row, picot, 7 d.c., picot, 4 d.c., and repeat from * all round the buckle ; slip-stitch into the first stitch and fasten off, securing the end of thread firmly on the wrong side of buckle.

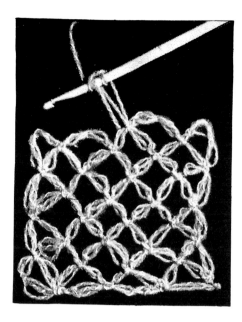

Hand=bag in Solomon's Knots.

Abbreviation : d.c., double crochet.

THIS is a smart and useful bag crocheted in Solomon's knot stitch, using any coloured macramé twine or coarse make of Ososilkie. It should be lined with silk, and if required as a stiff bag then it must be interlined with thin cardboard.

Materials : Strutt's Macramé Twine No. 8, and a No. o steel crochet hook, will make a bag about 8 inches wide.

Begin with 60 chain.

1st round—For the first knot draw out the chain on the hook until it is about half an inch long, thread over hook and draw through the loop, now insert the hook under the back thread of the three, draw thread through and make one chain ; this is called a half knot. Again draw out the loop on the hook until it is half an inch long as before and repeat the same stitch, miss five chain of the foundation, and put 1 d.c. into the sixth chain, thus completing the Solomon's knot. Repeat these knots right across the chain, then do another row of knots on the other side of the foundation, using the chains already worked into.

2nd round—Draw out the thread and work a whole knot as usual, then 1 d.c. into the double crochet in the centre of the next knot, and continue all round.

Repeat the second round until there are twenty-two rounds altogether, or more if a longer bag be desired.

Here begin the flap. Work knots exactly half way across the bag, * turn, do a half knot, 1 d.c. into the centre of first knot, and continue knots as before across the row. Repeat from * until there is only one knot in the row, and fasten off.

In the loops all round the flap work 8 d.c., taking the double crochet under two loops of the knot stitch.

Fold the flap over and across the top of the last long row at back of bag work double crochet, closely filling the loops ; turn with 2 chain, and work two more rows of double crochet, putting 1 d.c. in each stitch of last row.

The Button.—1st round—3 ch., miss two chain, 5 d.c. in the last chain.

2nd round—2 d.c. in each stitch.

3rd round—2 d.c. in each stitch.

4th round—1 d.c. in the first stitch, * 2 d.c. in the next stitch, 1 d.c. in next stitch, and repeat from * all round.

Repeat the fourth round until the piece is large enough to cover the button mould, then do a round of 1 d.c. in each stitch to contract the circle : fasten off, leaving a long thread hanging. Slip into the mould and secure by passing a few stitches from s de to side at back. Sew the button on bag, which is merely for ornament, as a snap fastener must be sewn under it.

For the Handle.—Make a length of chain about four times as long as the handle is required, then crochet this chain again in the usual way. Turn up the ends of the chain to make a loop, and sew a tassel at the joint as seen in illustration. Also make two more tassels for the corners of the bag. A tassel can be made by winding the twine twenty or more times round a book, tie very securely in the middle, then cut the twine in the centre opposite the tied end, and wind the end of string round the tassel about half an inch from the top to make the round ball.

SWEET PEAS.

White Star Sylko, No. 5, for flowers ; Green Star Sylko No. 5, for stems.

Make 6 ch., turn, miss 1, 1 d.c. in each of 4 ch., 3 d.c. in the next, work d.c. up the other side of foundation ch., 3 d.c. in stitch at the top. Work 4 more rounds of d.c. increasing at top and bottom of oval by putting 3 d.c. into 1 stitch. In the last row, along one side of oval only, work 2 d.c. into each stitch.

For the inside of flower, work a second petal in the same way, but work only 3 rounds so that the small petal will fit inside the larger one. This forms one flower. Work a second flower in the same way, and for the third work a petal like the inside of the larger flowers.

Double the flowers over, stitching the two parts together in the middle and having for the outside edge the full row, or the row with 2 d.c. in each stitch.

Join on the green to the middle of the flowers and work 4 little green leaves, with 4 ch., miss 1, 1 d.c. in each, catch down with a sl. st., Make a ch. 2 inches long and join to second large flower. Work 4 green leaves and then another ch. 2 inches long. Join to the small flower, with 4 green leaves, make a ch. for stem and finish off.

EVENING OR BOUDOIR SHOE IN IRISH CROCHET.

AT the present moment lace shoes are the most fashionable footwear for the boudoir or evening dress. Made in Irish crochet, they are very choice as well as serviceable, for the lace is made so that it can readily be removed from the shoe for the purpose of cleaning.

The shoe illustrated is in very fine bébé Irish crochet worked with Manlove's "Thread for Irish Lace," No. 80 for the principal part. For the edging and large roses on the instep, No. 42 was used; the berries were also made in the latter number. Manlove's "Unity" No. 10 was used for padding the large roses, this being the only part where any padding was employed.

THE MOTIF.

Fig. 1 shows how to commence the bébé motif. With the finer thread make 9 ch. and form into a ring, into which put 18 d.c., 1 d.c. into the first d.c., 6 ch., 1 d.c. into every third d.c. round, making 6 loops, into each loop put 1 d.c., 8 tr. and 1 d.c., round this row work another of 7 ch. and 1 d.c. into the vertical stitch on the back of the work between each petal, then into each of these loops put 10 tr. and a d.c. at the beginning and end. Make a third row in the same way on a row of 8 ch. loops, into each of which put 1 d.c., 12 tr. and 1 d.c.. Round this rose work a "filling" of double picot loops, putting one into the third tr. on a petal and another into the third last tr. on the same petal. The double picot loop is made thus:—9 ch., picot 6 of them by putting the hook through the third ch. and making a d.c., 8 ch., picot 6 of them by putting the hook through the second, and make a d.c., 3 ch., fasten as directed with a d.c. to the third tr. on the edge of a petal

in the rose. This gives 12 loops in the first row; the last of them must be fastened to the first between the two picots.

In the second row there are four "groups of trs." with two loops between them. After joining the last loop of first row to the first, work * 9 ch., fasten this with a d.c. to next loop between the picots (throughout), turn and work 9 d.c. on the 9 ch., turn again, and put 1 d.c. in last and 1 tr. into each d.c., 1 d.c. over the end of the loop. Now put a double picot loop into each of next two loops of last row and repeat from *.

In the third and each alternate row, fasten the last loop of preceding one to the first d.c. on the "group of trs." put another loop into the centre tr., and one in the last d.c., then one loop into each between the groups. In the fourth and each alternate row put the "group of trs." between the two loops over the preceding row. There are seven rows worked in this way round each rose. The "groups of trs." form the motif into a perfect square, of which nine are required for the shoe.

Having procured a pair of silk or satin evening shoes of any colour to match the dress, the shape for the crochet lace can easily be got by pinning (using very fine pins) a piece of soft muslin on the front part of the shoe, being very careful that it lies perfectly even and and uncreased over the satin. Pin all round the upper edge also round the edge next to the sole. When the front part is arranged, fit each side in the same way as far as the back where they meet. Crease, or mark all round the edge of the muslin, remove the pins, and cut out this shape (see Fig. 2) in strong calico. Mark a line up the middle of front, and place one of the motifs diamond-wise with this line as the centre, tack it in place carefully. At each of the upper sides of this motif tack another, allowing space for one row of the filling with which they are connected. Three more are tacked at each side and this should bring the work to the back in a number 5 shoe. Over the first motif

EVENING OR BOUDOIR SHOE IN IRISH CROCHET.

FIGURE I AND BERRY

EVENING OR BOUDOIR SHOE IN IRISH CROCHET.

with 4 ch. and work two more rows of 3 ch. and 1 d.c. in each loop, slip stitch down to next petal and repeat from *. Then take up the cord and work over it all round each petal, d.c. into the loops at each side, and into each loop on top 1 d.c., 5 tr. and 1 d.c.. Fasten off the thread on the back, and cut away the superfluous padding. Make another rose in the same way.

For the Berries. Form 3 ch. into a ring, work two rows of 2 d.c. into each stitch, then a row of 2 d.c. into every second d.c. and 1 d.c. into the alternate d.c.. Two rows of 1 d.c. into each, then a row of "narrowing" by taking up every second and third stitch together and making 1 d.c. through them, 1 d.c. through the intervening d.c.. After this row the berry will begin to "cup" and it is now filled with cotton wadding as closely as possible, then continue narrowing in the same way as before until only four stitches remain, take all these up on the hook with a loop through each and form a d.c. to close the berry. Make a length of three inches of chain stitches before breaking off the thread. Form three knots on the chain of

there will be a triangular space, this is filled with a single rose made like the others, and may require a row of filling at the lower part. Connect all the motifs with a row of the double picot loops by taking in the opposite loop in an adjoining motif between the two picots.

Make a "straightening" line of 1 tr. with 5 ch. between into each loop, using the No. 42 thread, round both edges. Remove from the foundation, and should the lace require it work a second row of 5 ch. and 1 tr. into each space round the lower side.

For the Top Edging. * 12 d.c. over the ch. (as close as possible), 8 ch., turn back and fasten to the seventh d.c., turn and into the loop put 3 d.c., 6 ch., 2 d.c., 6 ch., 2 d.c., 6 ch., 2 d.c., 6 ch., and 3 d.c., 5 d.c. on the straightening line, turn, 5 ch. and 1 d.c. into each picot, 5 ch., 1 d.c. into the third d.c. on the line, turn, 3 d.c., 6 ch. and 3 d.c. into each 5 ch. loop and repeat from *.

For the Large Roses on the Instep. Make a four-fold padding cord and insert the hook through the folded end, 15 d.c. over the cord, turn, join into a ring, and work two rows of petals as in former flowers but putting the d.c. and tr. over the cord instead of the ch. loops. Over the cord, after the second row of petals, work 10 d.c. only, for each, fastening as before, then leave the cord, * 3 ch. and 1 d.c. into every second d.c. on next petal, turn

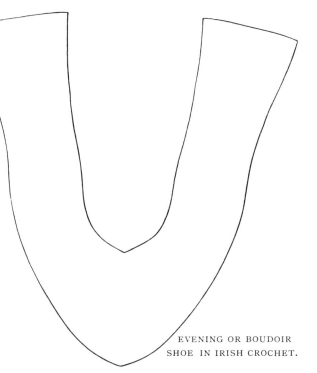

EVENING OR BOUDOIR SHOE IN IRISH CROCHET.

the stem by making a loop and slipping the berry through the loop, then pull up the loop into place.

After washing and pressing the lace, sew it with very neat small stitches to the edge of the satin shoe, commencing at the toe, next to the sole, turn in the edge of the lace as far as possible between the upper and sole with the point of the needle. It will render the work easier and perhaps more accurate if the lace is first tacked to the shoe. Sew the large roses at each side of the centre top rose, and taking three berries for each side sew the ends of the stems together, fasten behind the first rose and do the same for the other. The stems serve to tighten the shoe at the top if necessary, as they are tied in a bow knot on the centre.

"FOLKSTONE" CROCHET HAT.

Abbreviations: Ch., chain; sl.st., slip stitch; d.c., double crochet; tr., treble.

THE materials required for making the hat illustrated are:— One hank of Ardern's "Star Sylko" No. 3, Silver Grey, shade 718; a steel hook size 1, two yards of Millinery Wire; and one yard of Silver Grey Ribbon to match the "Star Sylko."

FOR THE CROWN.

Begin with 5 ch., join with a sl.st. into ring.

First row. 2 d.c. into each stitch; do not join the rows, but continue working into each stitch, round and round.

Second row. 2 tr. in each stitch, taking the upper loop.

Third row. Like the second.

Fourth row. 2 tr. in first stitch, * 1 tr. in each of the next 3 stitches, 2 tr. in next stitch, repeat from *.

Fifth row. 1 tr. in each of the first 4 stitches, 2 tr. in next stitch, * 1 tr. in each of the next 4 stitches, 2 tr. in next, repeat from *.

Sixth row. 1 tr. in each stitch all round.

Seventh row. 1 tr. in each of the first 5 stitches, 2 tr. in next stitch, * 1 tr. in each of the next 5 stitches, 2 tr. in next, repeat from *.

Eighth row. 1 tr. in each stitch all round.

Ninth row. Like the seventh.

Tenth row. Like the eighth.

Eleventh row. 2 tr. in first stitch, * 1 tr. in each of the next 6 stitches, 2 tr. in next, repeat from * to the end of round, and draw the thread through with a sl.st..

This finishes the crown, which should measure seven inches across.

FOR THE BAND.

Work 8 rows of tr. without any increase, beginning the first with 2 ch..

FOR THE BRIM.

First row. 2 ch., * 1 tr. in each of the next 7 stitches, 2 tr. in next stitch, repeat from *, join neatly to the 2 ch..

Second row. 2 ch., 1 tr. in each stitch all round.

Third row. 2 ch., * 1 tr. in each of the next 9 stitches, 2 tr. in next stitch, repeat from *.

Fourth and Fifth rows. 2 ch., 1 tr. in each stitch all round.

Sixth row. 1 d.c. in each stitch over wire.

The ends of the wire should be placed together, and firmly sewn, before being worked over.

Seventh row. Like the third.

Eighth row. Like the fourth.

Ninth row. Like the sixth.

Tenth row. 1 sl.st. in each stitch, join and fasten off.

The approximate number of stitches is given, but they may be increased or reduced at the discretion of the worker.

Cut a small piece off the ribbon, mount it on to a round of stiff material, and embroider with "Star Sylko," either size 3 or 5 in suitable colours. A small motif should be worked also on the band, and repeated according to the taste of the worker.

Lay the ribbon round the hat, cross the ends, and sew the disc firmly down.

Lady's Crochet Belt.

Abbreviations: ch., chain; d.c., double crochet.

MATERIALS: This belt is worked in coarse Ososilkie, or the coarse size of Peri-Lusta, or D.M.C. Coton Perlé No. 5 may be used, with a steel hook No. 2.

Our design measures 22 inches in length, and $2\frac{1}{4}$ inches in width. It is worked in blocks of double crochet, with lengths of chain between each block. The first and last blocks measure 3 inches each, allowing $\frac{1}{4}$ inch on each end for fixing buckles. The block on the back of the belt measures 4 inches, and those on either side $2\frac{1}{2}$ inches each.

The double crochet and chain must be worked tightly, so as to give firmness to the belt.

Begin by working 25 ch.

1st row—1 d.c. into the second chain from the needle, 1 d.c. into each of the next twenty-three chain.

2nd row—1 ch., 1 d.c. into first double crochet (take both threads of stitch all through blocks of double crochet), repeat 1 d.c. into each of next twenty-three double crochet of previous row. Work rows of double crochet till there are 3 inches for first block. Now work 45 ch., slip-stitch into first chain, 2 d.c. on block, * 45 ch., slip-stitch into first chain, 2 d.c. on block. Repeat from * till there are twelve lengths of chain with two double crochet between each length. After working last two double crochet work 23 ch., slip-stitch into twenty-third of first length of forty-five chain, 1 ch., ** slip-stitch into twenty-third of next length of forty-five chain, 1 ch. Repeat from ** into each of next ten lengths of chain. Turn, 1 ch., 1 d.c. into the twenty-third of the single length of chain last worked, 1 d.c. into each of next twenty-three stitches on the previous row. Turn, 1 ch., 1 d.c. into each double crochet on previous row. (Take both threads of stitch.) Work a second block of double crochet, measuring $2\frac{1}{2}$ inches, as directed. and then chain and blocks sufficient for the waist-belt.

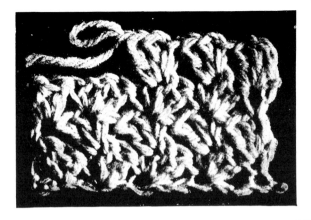

21

Lady's Sports Cap in Crazy Stitch.

Abbreviations : ch., chain ; tr., treble ; d.c., double crochet.

MATERIALS: 3 ounces of Faudel's "Pure Royal" Shetland floss and a No. o steel crochet hook.
This cap is composed of three-parts, each worked separately, two for the crown and one piece for the brim, and being light and elastic, can be stretched to fit the head. Begin with 25 chain.

1st row—2 tr. into the fourth chain from the hook, * miss two chain, 1 d.c. in the next chain, 2 ch., 2 tr. in the same place as double crochet, and repeat from * six times.

2nd row—One group, consisting of 1 d.c., 2 ch., and 2 tr. (all worked in the same place), must be increased at the beginning of this row, so, instead of putting the first group under the first two chain loop, put one in the first treble, thus, turn with 1 ch., 1 d.c. in the top of the very first treble (the last one worked in previous row), 2 ch., 2 tr. in the same place, * 1 d.c. under the two chain worked after the double crochet in previous row, 2 tr. in the same place, and repeat from * to the end of the row.

Repeat the second row ten times, when the crown will be sufficiently increased.

Work twenty rows without increasing, that is, at the beginning of the row work the first group under the first two chain loop instead of putting one extra group in the first treble, making thirty-two rows in all.

33rd row—At the end of this row decrease as follows : Work 1 d.c., 2 ch. under the last two chain loop as usual, but do not complete the group, simply turn after the two chain.

34th row—Work as usual under the first two chain loop, finishing the end of the row like the thirty-third row to decrease one group.

Repeat the last row eight times and fasten off.

Work a second crown piece exactly like this one, then place the two together and work double crochet right through the two pieces together. This completes the crown.

The brim is worked in one straight piece as follows :—

Make 166 chain and work fifty-six rows of groups in exactly the same pattern as crown, but without increasing or decreasing. This strip should measure about 24½ inches wide and 12½ inches deep.

Sew up the two shorter ends with a piece of the same wool to form a round. Fold up in half to bring the two edges together, place the edges of the crown between these two brim edges letting the crown go inside the brim for about half an inch to make the crown quite round ; stitch through as invisibly as possible with the same kind of wool, and fasten off securely. Fold up the brim again and the cap is complete.

22

NARCISSUS.

White Star Sylko No. 5, for petals ; Yellow and Black Star Sylko No. 5, for centre. Green Star Sylko No. 5, for leaves.

PETALS.—6 ch., turn, miss 1, 1 d.c. in each of 4 ch., 3 d.c. in 5th ch., turn, work along the other side of foundation ch., 1 d.c. in each, 3 d.c. in the stitch at the top. Work 2 more rounds of d.c., putting 3 d.c. in the stitch at the bottom and the same at the top, fasten off.

Work 5 more petals and join the ends together.

CENTRE.—2 ch. with yellow silk, miss the one nearest hook, and work 12 d.c. in the next, forming a circle. Join on black silk and work 1 ch., 1 sl. st., into every stitch. Stitch the little centre to middle of flower.

GREEN LEAVES.—Make a ch. about 6 inches long. Work d.c. along both sides of ch., putting 3 d.c. in top stitch and 3 d.c. in bottom stitch.

Make a second leaf in the same way about 4 inches long.

Stitch the two leaves together and place the flower about 2 inches away from the joining.

23

Crochet Buttons

Abbreviations.—Ch., chain ; d.c., double crochet ; r. st., roll stitch ; s.tr., short treble.

1st row.—Ring off 5 ch., 14 s. tr. in ring, s. st. to first st. Do not turn.

2nd row.—4 ch., 1 r. st. (thread 10 to 12 times over hook) in first s. tr. below, * 5 ch. 1 d.c. in fourth ch. from hook to form picot, 1 r. st. in next s. tr., 1 picot (but always make 5 ch.), 1 r. st. in same s. tr. as last, 3 ch. 1 r. st. in next s. tr. Repeat from * at end, 5 ch. (as picot), fasten to fourth ch. at beginning.

Flatter buttons can be made in thick silk or D.M.C. Coton Perlé, by working 15 s. tr. and putting 1 r. st. in each tr. ; this gives five groups of 2 picots instead of seven.

Pattern worked in Sylko, No. 16.

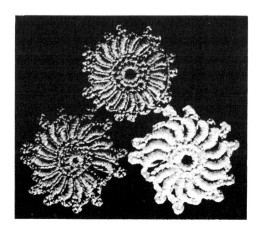

Lady's Crochet Gloves

Abbreviations : ch., chain ; d.c., double crochet ; tr., treble.

THESE most useful and quickly made gloves being crocheted in cotton are extremely durable, and wash splendidly, making an ideal glove for summer wear at the cost of a few pence.

If the finger-tips wear through they can easily be renewed by undoing the crochet half-way down a finger and working new tops.

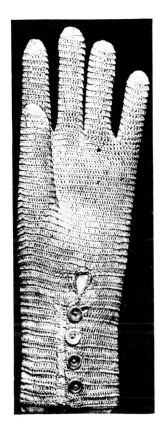

MATERIALS.

Two balls of Ardern's Lustrous Crochet Cotton No. 22 and a steel crochet hook size 4½ will make a pair of medium-sized gloves (6¼ to 6½ size). Ardern's Star Sylko No. 12, black or white, and a steel hook size 4½ may be used. A finer cotton, such as No. 26, would produce a smaller glove.

The work must be done loosely so that the glove is pliable. If a tight worker, a steel hook size 4 should be used.

FOR THE LEFT GLOVE.

Commence with 100 chain.

1st row—Miss three chain, 1 tr. into every remaining stitch, 3 ch., turn. This measures about 6½ inches.

2nd row—Miss the first treble, 1 tr. into every stitch, taking up two threads of the treble throughout the pattern, 1 tr. into the top of the chain that turned, 3 ch., turn.

3rd row—Same as 2nd row.

4th row—Miss one treble, 1 tr. into every stitch until the last seven are reached, 4 ch., miss four treble, 1 tr. into each of the three remaining stitches (this hole forms the buttonhole), 3 ch., turn.

5th row—Miss one treble, 1 tr. into every stitch (chain and treble), 3 ch., turn.

Repeat from commencement of 2nd row three times, when there will be four buttonholes made, 3 ch., turn work sideways and work along the ends of the seventeen rows, 3 tr. under the side of the treble last made, *3 tr. under end of next row ; and repeat from * to end ; 3 ch., turn. miss one treble, and work 1 tr. on each treble of previous short row, 3 ch., turn, miss one treble, 1 tr. into each treble of previous row, 3 ch., turn, miss one treble, 1 tr. into each treble of previous row ; these four rows form the small piece on which the buttons are to be sewn later on ; 3 chain.

18th row—Work along the ends of these four short rows, putting 3 tr. under each stitch at end of each row, then continue round the glove, putting 1 tr. into every stitch to end, 3 ch., turn.

19th row—1 tr. into very first stitch, 1 tr. into every stitch to end, 3 ch., turn.

Work three more rows like the 19th row, when the cotton will be at the buttonhole end of glove, then 3 ch., do not turn, but work 1 tr. into the first treble of previous row on opposite side of the wrist-piece, thus joining the two sides together, and the work will now proceed round and round to form the hand portion. The work should measure about 3¾ inches from the commencement of glove.

24th row—1 tr. into every remaining stitch, 3 tr. under the three chain which spaces across the opening of glove, then work 1 tr. into every stitch, including the three treble worked under the chain.

Now commence the shaping for the thumb.

25th row—1 tr. into each of the first twenty-two treble, 2 tr. into next treble, 1 tr. into each stitch to end.

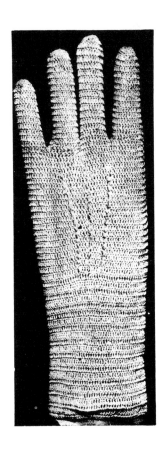

26th row—1 tr. into each treble until the first stitch of the two worked into same place is reached, then work 2 tr. into the first of these stitches, 1 tr. into next stitch, 2 tr. into next stitch, 1 tr. into every remaining stitch, 1 tr. into each stitch until the first treble of the two treble worked into one stitch is reached, 2 tr. into this stitch, 1 tr. into each stitch until the last treble of the next two treble worked into one stitch is reached, 2 tr. into this stitch, 1 tr. into every remaining stitch.

Continue working thus always putting two treble into the first stitch of the two worked into same place in previous row, then treble on treble, and 2 tr. into the last stitch of the last two worked into same place, until twelve rounds have been made, finishing on the last stitch of the two worked into one on thumb gusset. Now work 12 tr. after the last increase, fold the round together and work 1 tr. into the third stitch before the first increase on front of thumb gusset, thus making a small circle for the thumb, work round and round this small circle, putting 1 tr. into every treble of previous round for three rounds, then miss one stitch on the inside of thumb. Work three more rounds and miss one treble on inside of thumb. Work three more rounds, and then commence shaping the top.

10th row—* 1 tr. into each of the next five stitches, miss one treble ; repeat from * to end of round.

11th row—* Miss one treble, 1 d.c. into each of the next six stitches ; repeat from * all round ; then work 1 d.c. into each of the next four stitches, miss one stitch, and continue until there are only four stitches which almost close up the hole at top. Cut off the cotton about 9 inches from the work, pull the end through the loop to fasten off, then turn the thumb inside out, draw cotton through on to wrong side, and sew up the hole. Turn glove back on to right side, and commence again at the crutch of the thumb, and work 1 tr. into next stitch, 2 tr. under the side of the treble seen at right side of the opening, 1 tr. into next stitch, 1 tr. under side of next stitch, 1 tr. into same place as the treble just worked under, then 1 tr. into every stitch all round the palm.

(continued, p. 28)

(gloves, continued from p. 27)

Work nine rounds for palm, and finish the last round opposite to the place where the first treble was worked at the joining on after the completion of thumb.

1st finger—1 tr. into each of the next twenty-two treble, miss these twenty-two treble just made, also the next eight treble adjoining them, and span across to opposite side, making 1 tr. into next stitch; this forms the base of the finger; now work treble round and round for eight rows, miss one treble in next row, and work five more rows, then shape off the top of the finger in same manner as from 10th row of thumb. This finger measures 2½ inches.

Middle finger.—Commence at base of first finger, and work 1 tr. between the two stitches seen at opening at side of finger, 1 tr. under next treble, 1 tr. into same stitch on hand portion as treble just worked under, 1 tr. into each of the next thirteen stitches, span over to front of glove and work 1 tr. into the twelfth treble away from base of previous finger, keeping stitches on right side of work always, then work treble along these twelve stitches, 1 tr. under side of treble by opening, and continue now round and round for eight rows, miss one treble in next row, and work 6 more rows. Finish off top as usual.

Next finger—Work in same manner as previous finger, taking twelve stitches from each side of glove, and work round and round, making the finger the same as first finger.

Little finger.—Join on at base, and make the little finger on remaining stitches, doing six rows, then miss one treble and do five more rows and finish off as usual.

RIGHT GLOVE.

Work as for left glove to the end of the 23rd row, then 3 ch., take hook out of loop and insert it into top of the three chain at end of opposite side of piece (the buttonholes being at left side), take loop on hook, and draw it through the stitch. This joins the palm portions round, and the buttonholes are at left side at opposite side to first glove. Work 3 tr. under the three chain last made, and continue round for the palm until within twenty-three treble from end of round, 2 tr. into next stitch to commence the thumb gusset, 1 tr. into each of the last twenty-two stitches.

Next row—1 tr. on every treble until the stitch before the two worked into the same place is reached, into this stitch work 2 tr., 1 tr. on next treble, 2 tr. into the last stitch of the two worked into same place, and finish the round.

Now continue working round and round as for left glove, always putting two into the first of the two treble worked into one place and two treble into the last of the next group of two treble worked into one place, then work the thumb and fasten off.

Join on again at crutch of thumb as for left glove and work nine rounds for palm, finishing the last round opposite the place where the first treble was made for the joining of the thumb, work 8 tr. on next eight stitches, then miss these eight and twenty-two more stitches adjoining the eight, and work 1 tr. into next treble to join up and form the first finger, work round and round as for left hand. Fasten off.

Work other fingers as left hand, always joining cotton on for each new finger at base of last one made, and if it seems inclined to drag into a hole, put an extra treble between the fingers to make it strong.

Lastly work a row of double crochet all round top of glove and opening, putting 1 d.c. into each stitch along top, 3 d.c. at corner, 1 d.c. into each stitch along button portions, 2 d.c. into each stitch round opening at palm, 3 d.c. into each stitch up buttonhole side, and fasten off securely.

Sew buttons opposite the buttonholes, work the stitchings up back as in ordinary gloves, using the cotton double, and the gloves are ready for wear.

SINGLE DAHLIA.

Red Star Sylko, No. 5, for petals; Yellow Star Sylko No. 5, for centre; a No. 3 steel crochet hook is used for all the flowers.

PETALS.—Make 18 ch., turn, miss 1, 1 d.c. in each of 16 ch., 3 d.c. in the 17th ch., turn, and work along the other side of foundation ch., 1 d.c. in each 3 d.c. in last stitch. Work all round again with d.c., putting 3 d.c. in 1 stitch at each end, fasten off.

Work 10 petals and join all together, to form the flower.

CENTRE.—Cover a wooden mould with yellow silk, thus, 2 ch., miss the 1 nearest hook, work 12 d.c. in next ch., which forms a circle. Next row, 1 d.c., 2 d.c., alternately. Now work 1 d.c. into each stitch till the cover is large enough. Put it on the mould and draw the edges together at the back. Sew the centre to the flower.

The dahlia is intended to be worn flat on the crown of a hat, so each petal must be stitched in place.

Should the petals of any of the flowers be inclined to curl up press them out with a hot iron over a damp cloth.

The Rose Buckle.

Abbreviations: ch., chain; tr., treble; d.c., double crochet.

MATERIALS: Ardern's Star Sylko No. 3 and No. 8, a steel hook No. 4½, a darning needle, some millinery wire, and pliers.

The foundation for this buckle is made of millinery wire, which must be formed into an oval and the ends securely pinched together with the pliers; a bar must also be secured across the centre of the buckle shortways. The size of the buckle must be gauged by the number of roses desired round it; the roses worked with No. 8 Star Sylko will measure 1¼ inches across, and these would be suitable for a hat trimming. For a neck ornament small roses in crochet cotton or silk can be made, and the size of the buckle judged by the number of these small roses to be put round it.

With the Star Sylko No. 3 closely button-hole over all the wire, or a steel hook No. 2 may be used to work double crochet over the wire instead.

The Rose.—With the Star Sylko No. 8 and the No. 4½ steel hook make eight chain, which join into a ring with a slip-stitch.

1st round—6 ch. (three to stand for a treble), 1 tr. into the ring, * 3 ch., 1 tr. into the ring; repeat from * four times, 3 ch., and slip-stitch to third chain of the six with which the round commenced; there must be seven holes round the ring.

2nd round—Into each space work 1 d.c., 5 tr., 1 d.c.

3rd round 8 ch. (three to stand for a treble), 1 tr. into the first treble of first round, turn the petal of previous round forward so that the stitch can be easily picked up, * 5 ch., 1 tr. in next treble, and repeat from * all round, finishing with 5 ch., and slip-stitch into the third chain of the loop first worked.

4th round—Into each space work 1 d.c., 8 tr., 1 d.c.

5th round—10 ch., 1 tr. into first treble of third round, * 7 ch., 1 tr. in next treble, and repeat from * all round.

6th round—1 d.c., 10 tr., 1 d.c. in each space all round, and fasten off.

When working the second rose join to previous one in the last round as follows: Work 1 d.c., 5 tr., then slip-stitch into centre of corresponding petal on first rose, 5 tr. and 1 d.c. in same loop on second rose, and continue as usual. Join the last rose to the first one in the same way, then sew this loop of roses to the button-holed edge on the buckle as seen in illustration.

Crochet Yoke for a Lady's Nightdress.

THIS pretty yoke in worked in No. 36 crochet cotton. It is made in two parts, and these parts are worked in stripes. Cut a paper shape the size of yoke to be worked. Our design measures fourteen inches across the chest, eight inches from the shoulders to the first point, six inches from the shoulders to the second point. This measurement is without the edge.

❦❦❦

Begin with the **Insertion** on the right-hand side of the yoke.—Work 106 chain, turn, 1 treble into the fifth chain from the needle, * 1 chain, miss one chain, 1 treble; repeat from * forty-nine times. turn, 4 chain for long treble. 1 long treble into the second stitch, ** 2 chain, miss two chain, 2 long treble; repeat from ** twenty-four times, turn, 3 chain for treble, *** 1 chain, miss one chain, 1 treble; repeat from *** to the end of the row. This completes the insertion. Work all the other rows of insertion on the yoke in the same way. Now work the wheels.

❦❦❦

For the Wheel.—A ring of 6 chain.

❦❦❦

1st round—4 chain for long treble, * 4 chain, 1 long treble over the ring; repeat from * six times, then 4 chain, slip-stitch into the last of the first four chain.

❦❦❦

2nd round—1 double crochet, 5 treble, 1 double crochet all over the first space of four chain, 1 double crochet, 3 treble, 5 chain, slip-stitch into the last of the three treble, 2 treble, 1 double crochet all over the second space, 1 double crochet, 5 treble, 1 double crochet over the third space, 1 double crochet. 3 treble, 1 chain, 1 picot (five chain, slip-stitch into the first chain), 2 chain, 1 picot, 2 chain, 1 picot, 2 chain, 1 picot, 1 chain, slip stitch into the last treble, 2 treble, 1 double crochet all over the fourth space, 1 double crochet, 5 treble, 1 double crochet over the

(continued, p. 30)

(yoke, continued from p. 29)

fifth space, 1 double crochet, 3 treble, 5 chain, slip-stitch into the last treble, 2 treble, 1 double crochet over the sixth space, 1 double crochet, 5 treble, 1 double crochet over the seventh space, 1 double crochet, 3 treble, 1 chain, 1 picot, 2 chain, 1 picot, 2 chain, 1 picot, 2 chain, 1 picot, 1 chain, slip-stitch into the last treble, 2 treble, 1 double crochet over the eighth space. Finish off the thread firmly with a needle, work all the wheels on the yoke in the same way. Work a second wheel and join it to the first wheel, on the leaf where there should be a small ring of 5 chain, by drawing the thread through one of the small spaces of five chain. On the first row of the yoke have five and one half wheels. The half wheel is worked in the same way as the complete wheel, only working six long treble, and not completing the ring. Now work the squares on each side of the wheels, join the thread between the second and third picots on the half wheel, 3 chain, 1 treble into the same stitch, 19 chain, draw the thread through between the third and fourth picots on the same cluster as the thread was joined on, * turn, 1 chain, 1 double crochet into each of the first ten of the nineteen chain, turn, 1 chain, 1 double crochet into each of the ten double crochet (take the back thread of the stitch), turn, 1 chain, 10 double crochet, turn, 1 chain, 10 double crochet, turn, 1 chain, 10 double crochet, turn, 1 chain, 10 double crochet, 3 treble, working them all off together into the small space of five chain between the two wheels, turn, 1 chain, 10 double crochet, draw the thread through between the first and the second picots on the cluster on the top of the next wheel, slip-stitch up the side of the square of double crochet just completed and work 9 chain, 1 treble between the second and the third picots on the same cluster, 19 chain, draw the thread through between the third and fourth picots on the same cluster and repeat from *, working five complete squares on one side of the wheels and seven squares on the other side of the wheels. Begin the first of the seven squares by working 28 chain, draw the thread through between the first and second picots on the cluster of picots on the top of the first wheel, turn, 1 chain, 10 double crochet, 1 chain, 10 double crochet, 1 chain, 10 double crochet, 1 chain, 10 double crochet, 1 chain, 10 double crochet, 1 chain, 10 double crochet, then work 3 treble with the small space of five chain on the first wheel, 1 chain, 10 double crochet, slip-stitch up the side of the square, 9 chain, 1 treble between the second and third picots on the same cluster, then 19 chain and repeat as already described for the previous row. At the end of this row work seven chain (to begin the first point on the yoke), turn, work 1 chain, miss one chain, 1 treble to the end of the chain; repeat the same as on the previous insertion, increasing 3 long treble at the end of the row to form the first point on the yoke, then 1 row of 1 chain, miss one chain, 1 treble, increasing six spaces on the opposite end of the row for the neck. Work a second row of seven and a half wheels in the same way as the previous row of wheels, nine squares up the first side of the wheels. Join this row to the previous row of insertion by slip-stitching up the free side. Slip-stitch over the first nine stitches from the point on the yoke, then work one square, slip-stitch over the next nine stitches on the insertion, 1 treble between the second and third picots on the first cluster, slip-stitch over the next nine stitches on the insertion, 10 chain, seven rows of double crochet over this chain, 3 treble into the space of five chain between two wheels, draw the thread through between the first and second picots on the next clusters, and repeat the same as on the previous row. Work only seven squares on this row, and this will complete the first point on the yoke as well as begin to form the shoulder. Work a third row of insertion, and a third row of six and a half wheels, then a row of seven squares on the first side of the wheels, joining them to the insertion in the same way as described for the previous row, and work a row of six squares on the opposite side of the wheels. Increase 10 chain on the end of this row to begin the second point on the yoke. Work a fourth row of insertion. Lay the work from time to time on the paper shape. Work a fourth row of two complete wheels on the lower part of the yoke, and three half wheels on the upper part of the yoke. A row of six squares up the first side of this row, joining them to the insertion in the same way as already described, then one square between the two complete wheels on the other side. Now work a chain round the half yoke just completed. Join the thread to the first space on the front row of insertion, work 2 chain, 1 double crochet into the second row of chain, 4 chain, 1 double crochet into the third row, 2 chain, 1 double crochet into the fourth row of chain, 2 chain, 1 double crochet into the first picot, 2

(continued on p. 31)

A Motor Scarf

USE hook, No. 2 and Beehive Ivorine. Commence with 30 chain, then 1 tr. into the fourth stitch, * draw up the loop half-an-inch, put the silk over and draw through the loop, then work 1 d.c. on the line you drew through the loop, miss 3, then repeat from * until you have 24 holes of pattern, miss 3, then 2 tr. at the end and then turn.

2nd row.—3 chain, 1 tr. in the second stitch, then * draw up the loop as before and work 1 tr. in the centre of the d.c. Repeat from *. At the end work 2 tr. on 2 tr., that is, 1 on the tr. and 1 on the 3 chain which stand for a tr.

Work every row the same as you worked the *2nd row* until your work measures four feet long. This will just leave enough silk for the fringe each end.

For this, make 6 loops of the pattern, drawing it up 1 inch, then 1 d.c. on the work. This is clearly seen in the detail of stitches of scarf and fringe. Repeat until three dozen loops are worked, and finish the other end in the same way.

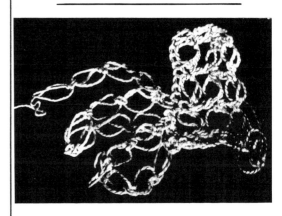

Detail of Stitches for a Silk Motor Scarf

chain, 1 double crochet into the next picot, 5 chain, 1 double crochet into the first free leaf on the first wheel, 5 chain, 1 double crochet into the next leaf, 5 chain, 1 treble into the first double crochet on the square, 8 chain, 1 treble into the last double crochet on the same square, 1 double long treble (thread three times over the needle) into the second space from the joining of the square to the insertion, 1 double long treble into the seventh space on the insertion, 8 chain, 1 double crochet over the last space, 8 chain, 1 double crochet over the last space on the next row of spaces, 8 chain, 1 double crochet into the last double crochet on the next square. (This completes the neck part.) Work down the shoulder with * 8 chain, 1 double crochet into the first double crochet on the same square, 6 chain, 1 double crochet into the first leaf, 5 chain, 1 double crochet into the next leaf, 5 chain, 1 double crochet into the next picot, 2 chain, 1 double crochet into the next picot, 6 chain, 1 treble into the second row of chain on the insertion, 5 chain, 1 double crochet into the last row of chain on the insertion, 5 chain, 1 double crochet into the first double crochet on the next square; repeat from * to the end of the shoulder. Round the arm work ** 6 chain, 1 treble into the first ring of six chain, 6 chain, 1 double crochet into the next leaf, 5 chain, 1 double crochet into the next leaf; repeat from ** to the last wheel on the arm, then 8 chain, 1 double crochet into the last double crochet on the last square. Work round the points *** 8 chain, 1 treble into the last double crochet on the square, 5 chain, 1 double crochet into the next leaf, 5 chain, 1 double crochet into the next leaf, 8 chain, 1 treble into the last double crochet on the next square, 2 chain, 1 double long treble over the eighth space from the point on the insertion, 1 double long treble over the fifth space on the insertion from the point, 10 chain, 1 treble into the point on the insertion, 5 chain, 1 treble into the same stitch, 10 chain, 1 long treble over the fourth space on the insertion from the point, 3 chain, 1 double crochet into the first picot, 2 chain, 1 double crochet into the next picot, 6 chain, 1 treble over the ring of six chain, 6 chain, 1 double crochet into the next leaf, 8 chain, 1 double crochet into the last double crochet on the next square, 8 chain, 1 double crochet into the two long treble on the insertion; repeat from *** round the second point. Work a row of 1 chain, 1 treble underneath the points, to sew the yoke to the material.

Work the second half of the yoke in the same way, turning the paper shape in the opposite direction. Sew the two half yokes to the material cut for the back of the yoke, and work a row of 1 chain, 1 treble, all round the neck. For the neck part work a stripe of wheels and squares the same as for the yoke, and join it to the space already worked on the neck, in the same way as the stripes were joined on the yoke. Round the top of the neck work a row of 1 chain, miss one chain, 1 treble.

The Edge.—**1st row**—Join the thread to the left-hand corner of the yoke, 4 chain for long treble, 1 long treble, 10 chain, miss two spaces on the yoke, * 1 double crochet over the next space, turn, 1 chain, 1 double crochet into each of the ten chain, turn, 1 chain, 1 double crochet into each of the ten double crochet (take the back thread of the stitch), turn, 1 chain, 10 double crochet, turn, 1 chain, 10 double crochet, turn, 1 chain, 10 double crochet, turn, 1 chain, 10 double crochet, miss two spaces on the yoke, 2 long treble over the next space, 10 chain, miss two spaces on the yoke; repeat from * round the two points on the half of the yoke up the front and round the neck, down the front of the other side, and round the next two points.

2nd row—Miss two double crochet on the first square, * 1 chain, miss one double crochet, 1 treble, 1 chain, miss one double crochet, 1 treble, 1 chain, miss one double crochet, 1 treble, 3 chain, 1 treble into the same stitch, 1 chain, miss one double crochet, 1 treble, 1 chain, miss one double crochet, 1 treble, 1 chain, miss one double crochet, 1 treble, miss two double crochet on the next square, 1 treble; repeat from * round all the squares on the edge.

3rd row—* 4 chain, 1 double crochet over each of the first three spaces, 4 chain, 1 double crochet over the same space, 4 chain, 1 double crochet over each of the next three spaces, 1 double crochet over the first space on the next square; repeat from *.

Up the front of the left-hand side of the yoke fill in the spaces between the squares in the following way:—

1st row—Join the thread to the two first free long treble on the neck, 4 chain for long treble, 1 long treble into the next long treble, * 6 chain, 1 double crochet into the point of the first free square, 6 chain, 2 long treble into the next two long treble, 6 chain; repeat from *.

2nd row—1 treble into each chain on the previous row.

3rd row—1 double crochet into each treble of the previous row.

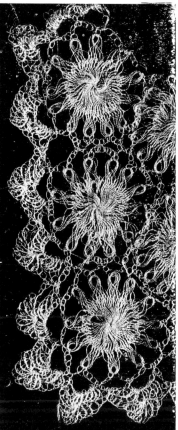

SHAWL.

THE shawl here illustrated is a new variety of the old-fashioned hair-pin crochet and is very light and lacey looking. Each wheel is made separately and afterwards joined together.

The materials required are 2 balls of Jevons & Mellor's (address Birmingham), 2-ply Eider Yarn, a bone crochet hook about the size used for Berlin wool, and a piece of *strong* wire, $9\frac{1}{4}$ inches long; this should be bent first at 4 inches then $1\frac{1}{4}$ inches farther on—this will form a large sort of hair pin. If it is not quite firm twist a finer piece of wire across a few times near the bent end.

Now begin the wheel in hairpin crochet with one strand of wool according to the illustration and continue until you have 60 loops on each pin. Then run a needle filled with wool through one set of loops (this is more easily done before drawing the crochet off the pins). Draw the work off pins and tie the needle and wool closely—this forms a wheel—then fasten the last stitch of crochet to the first and fasten off. Make a good many wheels before beginning to join together. It takes at least 12 in a row to make a small shawl. For joining, make a loop of wool on the crochet needle, then take up 5 outer loops of the wheel and crochet them together, work 6 chain and take up 5 more loops ; do this until you complete the circle and there should be 12 sets of loops, fasten off. In joining

(continued, p. 32)

(shawl, continued from p. 31)

second wheel to first, begin with one set of 5 loops, and then instead of 6 chain work only three and work a joining stitch into one of the loops of chain stitch of the first wheel, * then 3 more chain, now take up the next 5 loops of the wheel you are working, then 3 more chain. Join into the next row of chain of the first wheel, repeat from *. After making the third joining to first wheel finish the circle round the wheel, with 6 chain and working 5 loops together, etc. This has to be repeated with each wheel until you have enough wheels in a row to make the shawl the size required.

Joining the next row of wheels is more difficult, but with the help of the illustration I hope to make it clear. Make a beginning as you did with the other wheels by taking 5 loops, then 3 chain, join into the row of chain, second to right of where the first set of wheels were joined, then 3 chain, take up 5 more loops, then 3 chain, and join into row of chain next to the one just joined, 3 chain, 5 more loops, 3 chain and join into the same row of chain as the one where the wheels of the first row were joined, 3 chain, 5 more loops, 3 chain and join into row of chain of the next wheel of first row. Repeat this twice more so that there are six joins altogether, three into number one wheel and three into number two wheel, making sure that the third and fourth joining go into rows of chain, where there is already a joining. If you do not work it thus, the wheels will not be close together but will have an ugly hole between. As the wheels are six-sided, one row of wheels fits between the other row like a honey-comb. If it is found difficult to join this way, the shawl can be made of rows of wheels and then the rows afterwards secured together with ice wool.

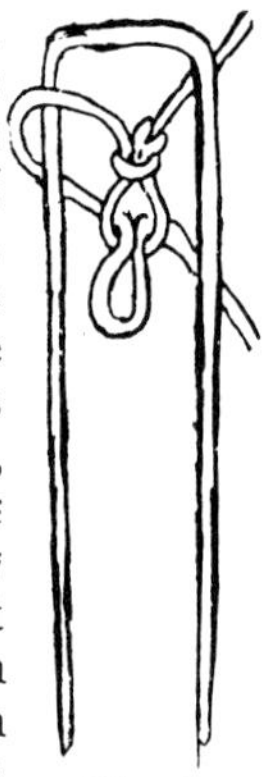

Fig. I

For the border, make * one double into edge of wheel, 10 chain, work one double into the wheel farther on, 10 chain again * repeat all round the shawl.

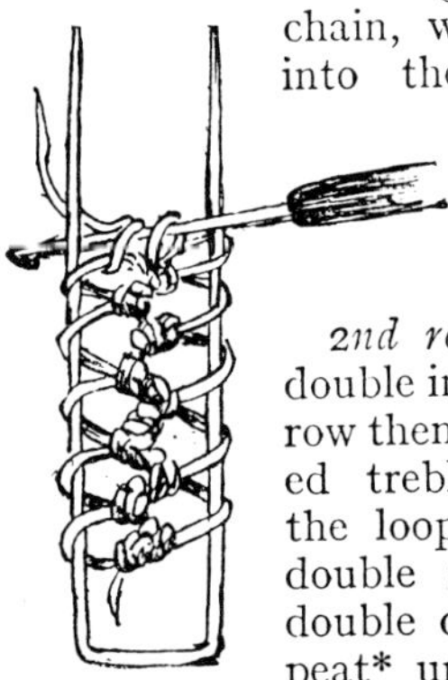

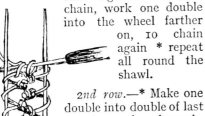

Fig. II.

2nd row.—* Make one double into double of last row then 10 loosely worked treble crochet into the loops of last row, 1 double again into next double of last row, repeat* until you go all round the shawl.

3rd row.—* 1 double in double of last row, 3 chain, 8 loose trebles into the top of number 5 treble of last row, 3 chain, and repeat from *.

(hooded cape, continued from p. 10)

through a treble stitch of each row, wool over the hook, and draw the wool through the 3 loops on the hook, work thus, working into each stitch till all are joined together and the elastic in the case; sew the ends up to keep the elastic in place, and then pass it through the spaces at the neck, putting the case with the with the elastic through one and over the next space. Sew one end to each corner of the neck, and for the strings. With the hook, No. 11, make a chain the length required (about 100 stitches). Work 1 treble into each chain stitch, and to round the end of the string work 6 treble into the first chain stitch, and then up the second side work 1 treble into each stitch. 2nd row—* 1 double, 4 chain, miss 1 stitch, repeat from * all round the two sides and end. 3rd row—1 double over the 4 chain of the last row, * "picot" (a "picot" is worked thus, 3 chain, 1 double into the first of the 3 chain) 1 double over the next 4 chain, repeat from * all round the two sides and the end. Fasten off the wool. Work a second string the same, sew the strings with a piece of the wool to each end of the elastic at the neck.

For the Hood.—Make a chain of 104 stitches and work the pattern the same as the wrap, till there are 6 patterns of 8 rows each worked. Then to shape the hood decrease 1 stitch by working 2 stitches together at the beginning and end of the 1st and the 5th rows of each pattern till 5 more patterns are worked, when there should be 88 rows worked and 84 stitches across the row. 89th row—in this row the shaping for the neck is commenced—decrease 1 stitch, 30 double, turn back (this completes the 1st row of the neck) and work backwards and forwards till one side of the neck is finished. 2nd row—decrease 1, 28 double, turn back. 3rd row —29 double turn back. 4th row—decrease 1, * work a "tuft," 3 double, repeat from * 6 times more, turn back. 5th row— decrease 1, 26 double, turn back. 6th row—decrease 1, 25 double, turn back. 7th row—26 double, turn back. 8th row—decrease 1, * 3 double, a "tuft;" repeat from * 4 times more, 4 double, turn back. 9th row—decrease 1, 24 double, turn back. 10th row—decrease 1, 23 double, turn back. 11th row—decrease 1, 22 double, turn back. 12th row—1 double, * a "tuft," 3 double; repeat from * 4 times more, 1 double, turn back. 13th row—decrease 1, 20 double, turn back. 14th row—decrease 1, 19 double, turn back. 15th row—decrease 1, 18 double, turn back. 16th row—decrease 1, a "tuft," 3 double; repeat from * 3 times more, 1 double, turn back. 17th row—decrease 1, 16 double, turn back. 18th row—decrease 1, 15 double, turn back. 19th row—decrease 1, 14 double, turn back. 20th row—decrease 1, a "tuft," 3 double, a "tuft," 3 double, a "tuft," 4 double, turn back. 21st row—decrease 1, 11 double, turn back. 22nd row—decrease 1, 10 double, turn back. 23rd row—decrease 1, 9 double, turn back. 24th row—decrease 1, 1 double, a "tuft," 3 double, a "tuft," 2 double, turn back. 25th row—decrease 1, 7 double, turn back. 26th row—decrease 1, 6 double, turn back. 27th row—decrease 1, 5 double, turn back. 28th row—decrease 1, 4 double, turn back. 29th row—decrease 1, 3 double. Fasten off the wool. For the second side of the neck work on the last 32 stitches of the 89th row to correspond with the first side, working the rows forwards and backwards, and being careful to work the "tufts" so that they come in their proper places. Cut the silk the shape of the crochet just worked for the hood, and then sew in place, putting the silk on the wrong side of the hood, and having tacked it neatly together, fold the hood-piece together and sew up with a piece of the wool, commencing from the *ends* of the foundation chain to the centre of it, having first joined the silk on the wrong side; then hem the silk neatly to the crochet round the neck and edges. Sew on the silk cord from the *points* at the neck, so as to conceal the stitches where it was joined together.

Frill for the neck.—With the crochet hook, No. 5, make a chain of 65 stitches, and for the first row work 6 *long* treble stitches into *each* stitch of the chain. 2nd row—on the second side of the foundation chain 1 treble stitch into each chain stitch, without breaking off the wool; work * 1 double into the first or next of the long treble stitches, working through both loops of the stitch; ** a "picot," miss 1 stitch and repeat from * all across the row. Fasten off the wool—using the wool double, thread a rug needle, and gather the frill to the size of the neck part of the hood and sew it on— and then sew the hood to the wrap. ** A "picot" is worked thus, 3 chain, 1 double into the part of the 3 chain.